8/20/16

Gregg —
go for the
cultural
magic !

Sara

THE POWER OF
INTERNAL MARKETING

THE POWER OF INTERNAL MARKETING

BUILDING A VALUES-BASED CULTURE IN CORPORATE AMERICA

By LAMAR D. BERRY

Good Reading Books • New Orleans, Louisiana

ISBN 1-888042-07-9

DEDICATION

To Jason F. Berry, Sr., a country boy from Arkansas who traveled the world during World War II, later settled in New Orleans, and became a storyteller to his children. In business as in private life he was an example of moral values. Also, to my brother Jack, an audio engineer, whose companionship helped brighten the tone of my dad's last months of Alzheimer's.

ACKNOWLEDGMENTS

Without the involvement of Ray Knight, this book would not have made it to publication. Ray is our chief strategic scribe at International Marketing Systems and is an important pillar of our young culture. Thanks.

Thanks also for conceptual and editorial help from my always interested mother — a most reliable literary and grammatical critic — Mary Frances Devine Berry and my brother Jason Berry, an accomplished author, for whom I have tremendous respect and admiration on a number of fronts. Thanks to both of you.

Over the last twenty-five professional years I have been blessed with having many milestones occur during the journey. When my career has encountered change, something magical has lit the pathway. The combined wisdom, guidance, and support of (or simply exposure to) a number of people or companies has to be recognized, for it has helped create my experiential melting pot. I want to thank:

William Perry Brown Jr., Popeyes Fried Chicken (A. Copeland Enterprises), Tom Feltenstein (past chairman of ARMG for being there after Popeyes), Patrick Terhune (for being there, shortly after ARMG), Bob Berkowitz, Texaco, Walt Disney World, Valerie Oberle, and my great friend and strategic co-conspirator, Ron Lewis.

Our host for this book, the carrier that has made it possible, is International Marketing Systems. My thanks to other IMS Executive Committee members for contributing to and believing in our vision: Gary Dickson, Rob Sanders, Kathy McNamara, Mickey Caplinger, Steve Conroy (corporate counsel), Sally Rodman, Rick Skaugh, and Melissa Wilson.

The support team at IMS has been essential. They are seeing the light and are so creative and special. Particular thanks to:

Patrick Donovan (who helped considerably during the later stages of preparing this text for publication), Amanda Collier, Sarah Dwyer, Jennifer

Guidry, Mike Karkowski, Jeff Lewis, Allison McInnis, Zarin Miller, Jennifer Powell, Pam Risey, Karla Schwem, and Vanessa Smit.

My wife Ellen and son Zachary (12) have spent numerous evenings and weekends watching Dad "work on the book." Thanks for your patience.

And most of all, thanks to IMS's clients. Without the ongoing experiences (both ups and downs) they have availed me, this commentary on corporate culture would not be remotely possible. It is within their real worlds of the free trade marketplace where human enterprise is being played out.

FOREWORD

International Marketing Systems, the company I endeavor to lead, works with many corporations. We create internal marketing systems. That is, we assess the internal philosophical and emotional dynamics of the employees of our clients and help them boost profits by strengthening their corporate cultures and service delivery systems.

In 1989 I was surveying a situation for Texaco Latin America/West Africa that involved their international chain of service stations. Jim Hawn, the Division's director of marketing at the time, and I landed in Bogota, Colombia. The country is notorious for drug lords and cocaine cartels. Jim's position with the global oil giant prompted the President of Texaco, Colombia, to have a welcoming contingent greet us at the airport. This small, most-hospitable group was joined, in turn, by an armor-plated limousine, two armed agents (with "uzis" no less) to accompany the "lead" Jeep (to lead us around), and two more "agents" for the "trail" jeep (to see where we were going).

I was told by their security chief not to think much of it for we had not given local management much advance notice of our visit. Ergo, any currently irritated criminals or terrorists hadn't had enough time to plot chaos. "It takes a solid couple of months to prepare a good kidnapping, you know."

In this political environment Colombia had somehow become the home of the friendliest, most service-oriented gas station in the world. And it had the sales to prove it!

There, in the town of Medellin, close to the back jungles of one of the most mob-infested developing countries in the hemisphere, stood a Texaco service station that would have made Milton Berle or Bob Hope beam.

If you don't remember, those vintage entertainers were once commercial spokesmen for Texaco. They hark back to the "good old days" of petroleum products marketing when retail outlets were truly service stations rather than mere filling stations. It was a time of Americana, when singing gas attendants on TV symbolized service standards that one had grown to expect.

So there I was — a baby boomer nurtured on fast food, pop culture and soundbite news — trying to understand the anomaly of record-breaking performance from a retail gasoline outlet in a global backwater where one of the main uses for cars seemed to be shielding oneself from random gunfire. Albeit, not likely in reality, but certainly in perception.

After surveying the business for awhile, the reason for such superior performance became clear — stellar service. This Texaco station operator, Aurelio Mejia, captured the kind of service magic that has become a hallmark of another company which features a special kind of magic — the Disney organization. I was there to study, learn, and potentially start cross-pollinating concepts for Texaco.

Mister Mejia does this by involving all his employees — the pump attendants, mechanics and cashiers — in making a connection with his customers. Not just in pumping the gas and ringing up the sale, but in making the connection. Service and the personal motivation therewith have become a part of his small company's culture, a natural part of the organization.

Several years later, when I was working with the senior marketing executives of Texaco U.S., they too identified the importance of focusing on and building stronger "connections" throughout their first-world distribution and retailing network.

With corporations, as with all organizations, the culture should work on behalf of a common good. When people at the top are disconnected from those in the middle and across the broad working level of a company, the operation may well make money, but it's unlikely to achieve its potential. Smart companies continuously stay aware and on top of this cultural connection.

And here you find the challenge. The culture of your company should work for you, not against you. Whether it's in Panama City, Panama, or Panama City, Florida, the mindset of the employees should be joined to a clear corporate mission.

What do I mean by stressing that a company's culture should work for you? Let's look at our remarkable friend in Medellin.

Developing countries are notorious for choked infrastructures and substandard services. What was Mister Mejia doing? How was he doing it? And what can we learn from it?

This dynamic entrepreneur actually bought the house next door to his service station to use as a customer service training center for his operation. Over time his employees turned into an appreciative group of believers. They internalized his values, chief of which was total customer satisfaction. To Mister Mejia, customer satisfaction is an obsession, not a slogan. He motivates his staff by taking them on exploratory weekend field trips, where they analyze the service strengths and weaknesses of any retailer from whom they can learn, not just the competition in their own oil-and-gasoline category.

Mister Mejia stages holiday events on his "forecourt" (driveway), inviting employees and customers to costume, mingle and party. He also created a computer database marketing program that reaches his customers throughout the hinterlands of Colombia. Monthly themed promotional offers keep his traffic count constant.

We produced a video on this intrepid entrepreneur. Texaco has shown the tape at meetings far and wide in developing countries. There are certainly lessons to be learned here. When Mr. Mejia took over his service station in the early 1980s, it was selling 30,000 gallons of gasoline per month. By 1990, he was selling over 300,000 gallons per month, plus tens of thousands of dollars in car repair and lubricant sales. A superstore has mushroomed around his service station. The message to South American operators — and to those in Central America and West Africa (where IMS also does business with Texaco) — is straightforward. If Aurelio Mejia can do it, why not you?

Undoubtedly, Aurelio Mejia is a natural salesman. But he is also an embodiment of the culture-of-quality — a mentality that shapes the operating sensibilities of high-profile models of success such as Walt Disney World, Federal Express and Ritz-Carlton.

Aurelio Mejia has created his own paradigm, a universe that moves to his impressive drumbeat. The answer to how he did it is simple, yet absolutely challenging and difficult to pull off. He insisted on commitment, communication and care from everybody.

Commitment to his goal of operating the world's best Texaco station. Communication of his vision and daily expectations to his team of employees. And care for his employees (as if they were family) and for his customers (letting them know, in subtle and courteous ways, that he can't live without them).

How does his culture work? Notice the word care. He's not manipulating his people. Hence, they aren't manipulating each other. He's in there sharing their experiences as they grow, leading his employees by identifying with them in a common quest: a stronger company, paying better wages as profits climb. He's the owner, but they are stakeholders in the prosperity or decline of the enterprise.

By contrast, far too often in corporate America we find employees functioning with little if any exposure to organizational values at the top. Corporate culture is hardly alone in this respect. Alienation of voters from elected officials has been a constant theme of the political pundits. This lack of bonding with the principles and character of the employer is, as the Tofflers put it, not just a "third wave" information-age phenomenon. It has been evolving since commerce progressed out of the simpler agrarian age and thrust our daily relationships into industry, decentralized businesses and distant communications.

This disassociation in the business world has its parallels in the much-discussed loss of moral fiber in society. The reasons are complex and multifaceted. My purpose in this book is not to explore the many causes of society's ills. As a businessman, I am disturbed by the loss of focus and mutual trust in the business world. I see it as *the great disconnect* — the loss of a common bond between employees (among themselves) and with their employers. Its by-products are loss of commitment, integrity, and productive performance in the workplace.

Every organization has a culture and an operating ethos. The culture evolves from a company's origins and founders; it is not static. Many things affect its evolution. A corporation can experiment, shift its base of operations, engage in a large-scale retraining, downsize, or decide to resist a given trend.

All of these concerns spring from the paradigm, or model for procedures and philosophies, that help make up the corporate culture. It is humanizing for an institution when its personnel have access to upper management's vision; it is psychologically rewarding for employees to know that they are valued as people and are conceptual stakeholders in the common enterprise. Organizational values affect performance. And performance affects sales.

At issue is the heart of an organization, what makes it operate, what directs its flow of energy, its dynamism and purpose. And in this sense, executives directing a business's pathway cannot conveniently hide behind the fabled "corporate veil." They are people running an enterprise consisting of people. And if, in Colombia, Aurelio Mejia can capture a sense of purpose and integrity within his company by educating, indoctrinating and motivating his work force to achieve superior performance, surely the visionaries of corporate America can work to correct a paradigm crisis in the information age.

TABLE OF CONTENTS

PROLOGUE

BEYOND TQM

BEYOND TQM
Service is not Manufactured

W. Edwards Deming contributed significantly to the manufacturing world through his insightful *quality process.* However, our emerging *service generation,* which is so retailing-driven, is getting quite confused over it. What works in one landscape (say, a manufacturing plant) will not necessarily work in another (a restaurant or a casino).

The instantaneous nature of the eye-to-eye human interaction called *service* is a very emotional and psychological phenomenon. Look at the world of consultants — it's full of Total Quality Management (TQM) sages trying to force the Deming square peg into the retail world's round hole. I call for introspection before we take that process too far. In this case, I believe that the cure is worse than the ailment.

The spiritual and cultural values of past corporate traditions and organizational cultures are not thematic or convenient to the TQM foundations.

Quality as a philosophy is unassailable. But beware of those who attempt to overlay a manufacturing-generated concept onto a retail service-driven paradigm in order to produce enhanced "customer service."

They know not of what they speak.

For the most part I fear they are business mercenaries trying to expand their current marketplace or protect their jobs. This reminds me of an encounter I had with a hospital human resources vice president. We were at a professionals' service seminar. She announced to me over eggs one morning that the health care industry was *paradigm shifting* from supply to service. And although that seemed right up my company's alley, she warned me of the inevitability of all suppliers in health care ultimately having to be *ISO 9000 certified*. This, she insisted, will some day include International Marketing Systems. If we wanted health care clients in the future, we'd better get on the "Quality" bandwagon.

The Deming diehards have little appreciation for the corporate culture that must endure to manifest superior performance in the service sector. Many are blindly following a quality cult.

As I later pondered this thought, the frightening reality dawned on me of just what the Deming diehards were striving to accomplish. They have digested little about the inspiration and internal emotion required in superior, retail customer service. They have little appreciation for the corporate culture that must endure to manifest such superior performance. Many are blindly following a quality cult.

What they do appreciate is a type of sacred ground on which they stand. They find comfort in the manufacturing philosophies which they know and discomfort with the philosophies of categories that they don't know. They respect the functional realities of the present day. In this sense they are mostly gnostic in their views. The spiritual and cultural values of past corporate traditions and organizational cultures are not thematic or convenient to the TQM foundations.

How unguided the quality movement has been as it has tried to expand its grasp into the service sector. In their current day's quest, the importance rests in having ISO 9000 certify a machine or, greater yet, certify the entire manufacturing plant. And don't forget all of the folks who supply those plants' smaller parts. *Let's certify all the suppliers. What a godsend; we can certify the world! Think of the pyramid of quality consultants and certifiers we can create!*

Alas, many of the human resource folks of the '70s and '80s are carving out exciting relevance for the twenty-first century. By tomorrow, they'll try (unsuccessfully, I predict) to certify the spirit.

A mass of yesterday's human resource people are now disciples of TQM. They shifted with the tides when Deming's process offered more fertile opportunity in a job market being reconstructed by a constantly changing and somewhat unappreciative industrial and manufacturing arena. There was new-found value and security in the "quality" they offered.

Today, we are experiencing more focus and emphasis being placed on the service sector; integral to this category is retail.

The TQM people need to be up to a challenge. They need to better understand the retail/service paradigm or continually confront the frustrating obstacles of trying to overlay their assembly/production mentality onto the moving target of vitally different environments.

Karl Albrecht in his book *The Only Thing That Matters* has an entertaining tale describing the concept of paradigm. It reads:

> A story surfaced just after the close of the Second World War in Europe about a Russian soldier who was part of the Soviet force that moved into Berlin to set up the occupation of the city. According to the story, the soldier entered a German house and saw an electric light for the first time in his life.
>
> Fascinated by this magical gadget — this light bulb hanging from the ceiling at the

end of an electrical cord — he decided he had to have it. He drew his bayonet, cut the wire off at the ceiling, and tucked the device into his knapsack. Presumably, he intended to take it back to his native land, hang it from the ceiling, and enjoy its magical benefits. Unfortunately, he knew nothing of the theory behind the existence of the light bulb. He didn't know about power plants, transmission lines, transformers, fuse boxes, wires running through walls, or light switches. He just knew that this marvelous gadget produced light.

The service/retail sector culminates in an experiential, emotionally inspired, one-on-one, human performance.

This story frequently comes to mind when observing company executives in their attempts to capture the magical essence of service quality by trying to imitate one of the legendary service companies. Lacking the frame of reference for thinking about service quality, they go around cutting down light bulbs and taking them home. The executives want to imitate Nordstrom or Disney or Marriott or Federal Express. They don't understand that they must learn a whole new frame of reference in order to light their own corporate houses. Just like the soldier, they're having *paradigm problems.*

The quality pundits are a smart group. If their goal is to market their skills into numerous business categories, they must understand those category paradigms. Unlike a light bulb and electrical generating plants, the service/retail sector culminates in an experiential, emotionally inspired, one-on-one, human performance.

In this human service ballet of sorts, TQM and Malcolm Baldridge should not be the fulcrum of the process, let alone the source of the lexicon. It is a matter of too much process and too little culture.

The world of retail is where *service* and one's goods come into personal sales contact with a customer. It is a dynamic and potentially magical encounter; it can actually make both parties feel good about themselves. It involves restaurants and service stations — but, increasingly, retailing is a mindset being embraced by less readily identifiable categories such as utility and phone companies, banks and hospitals.

If hospitalized, I certainly will rest more comfortably knowing that my EKG machine and I.V. have been ISO 9000 certified. However, I doubt if I'll take any notice or let alone experience any uplifted emotions if my robotic-like nurses aide follows his sixteen-step Customer Satisfaction process in order to retain some displaced sort of ISO 9000 service certification.

In service industries, the voice of a front line worker should reveal a believer — one who holds a belief not just in the job, but in the way that customers are treated by the company.

So, as the lines of demarcation between manufacturing/supply and retail/service become more obscured, care must be taken when dealing with the emotion and soul of the workplace. In service industries, which are more dependent than many others on spontaneous interactions among people, management succeeds when it fosters a sense of personal worth among those who deal directly with the customer. This is especially apparent in video rental stores, convenience stores, department stores, various retail outlets, and casinos. In all of these environments, the voice of a front line worker should reveal a believer — *one who holds a belief not just in the job, but in the way that customers are treated by the company.* You see these believers behind the counters at McDonald's. You see them among the cast members at

Disney World and Disneyland. You see them on the staff at Ritz-Carlton hotels. You see them handling packages at Federal Express.

It takes much work and time, but even in today's chaotic climate it is possible to create order, discipline, and commitment in an organization's attitudes and philosophies. *People by nature want to belong.* It is possible to create *believers.* While ISO certifications and TQM specialists have their role, they are not as essential for service companies (in their quest to exceed customer expectations) as is having believers. TQM can help track the upper and lower control limits of a production process, but don't count on it to produce a process that enhances employee vitality and productivity in the retail service sector. That's a *cultural issue.*

CHAPTER

CRISIS IN CORPORATE AMERICA

CRISIS IN CORPORATE AMERICA
The Great Disconnect

Yesterday's rules don't work today, and today's norms might be replaced as quickly as tomorrow. The life span of new technologies has shortened to months (even weeks) instead of years or decades. In the tumult, employees experience the great disconnect. Companies are growing disconnected from their roots.

To master the pace of change, corporate America must be guided by clear vision and solid values.

General society and the corporate world are vitally linked, yet on the eve of the 21st century, most companies struggling to keep up with change make decisions reactively, not strategically. To master the pace of such swift change, corporate America must be guided by clear vision and solid values. All too often American businesses lack a values-based working ethos. This writer has been privileged to work with a number of enterprises whose standards are laudable.

My career has also shown me that companies without a strong root system of values risk being snapped off at the stem, like tumbleweeds, and pushed along at the whim of environmental winds.

AN IMAGE OF STABLE VALUES
As the information age takes root, the rate of change in the workplace is marked by astonishing speed and a climate of volatility. No business world has ever been

No business world has ever been angelic, but there was a time in living memory when companies large and small were perceived as safety zones for people entering the job market. The general public believed in them.

angelic, but there was a time in living memory when companies large and small were perceived as safety zones for people entering the job market. The general public believed in them. You could trust your car to the man who wore the star at Texaco. You could furnish your house and clothe your family by mail order from the Sears & Roebuck catalogue — knowing that if it wasn't right, Sears would make it right. You knew that Ivory Soap was 99 44/100 percent pure.

Young people went to work for companies and stayed with them loyally until retirement. People could dependably plan their futures — buy homes and raise families with a promise of stability and shared values among home, church, school, and other institutions.

DESTABILIZATION

World War II erased the cataclysm of the Great Depression, and people who had gone through the war looked forward to renewed prosperity. For a while they seemed to have it. Then in the '60s, social stability began to unravel. The civil rights upheaval, reaction to the Vietnam war, and emergence of the drug subculture began to undermine assumptions of the majority. Polarization in America grew on a scale not seen since the Civil War. Social institutions were challenged and defied. American flags, banks, school buildings, and whole sections of cities were burned. So began a destabilization of the structures that bind our society together.

The signs of disconnection continued through the Seventies and Eighties: Watergate, Iran-Contra, sports scandals involving drugs and gambling, Wall Street thievery, and sex abuse in the home, school, and church filled the news. Heroes and institutions suffered in reputation; the idea of individual privacy eroded. By the mid-nineties, television viewers were begging for a vacation from talk shows about cross-dressers and those with foot fetishes. Television network programmers seemed so obsessed with vulgarity and images of "America the bizarre" that political figures like William Bennett publicly suggested that sponsors of advertising time rethink media buys for their products on certain programs. It was in this climate of excess that legislation for the "V-Chip" gained support.

PEOPLE ARE THE REAL HEART OF A COMPANY

In corporate America the leveraged buy-out (LBO) rage magnified the disconnect. When the LBO massacre ripped out the hearts of many American companies, the hearts of employees and their families went too. Corporate raiders butchered the carcasses of their takeovers and sold off the parts like cuts of meat — it was handled that impersonally. However, I have always believed that behind every perceived problem is an opportunity; unfortunately, our business leaders slept through this one.

With some notable exceptions, what was left was a business world that had lost face before the general public and emerging employable youth. As one college student put it, "I should view employment as the chance to get in, get mine, and then move on to something better." Others were not so cynical. Like politicians, corporations were being held to a new standard of conscience as perceived by non-employees and disparate interest groups who were willing to create havoc in a destabilized workplace. Interest groups abound today, and American business is frequently judged by a particular measure of public responsibility and employee reaction. For instance, companies known for their civic service can be tarnished by events at their overseas operations, provoking immediate protests that make for damaging news. Any group can become Gulliver to the Lilliputians. The media lets it be so. Even if, in reality, it is only a special interest group of two — proclaim your group, call the press, and fire up the Internet! You, too, can destabilize!

THE SEEDS OF ANOMY

In his work on ethics, the 19th century sociologist Emile Durkheim identified a sinister by-product of specialization in the workplace — anomy.

Long before the Information Age arrived, the Great Disconnect germinated in the divisions of labor in the late middle ages. In his work on ethics, the 19th century sociologist Emile Durkheim identified a sinister by-product of specialization in the workplace — anomy (or anomie in Durkheim's native French). Anomy was defined in the Oxford English Dictionary of the time as "disregard of the law" and "lawlessness." In an 1893 treatise, *The Division of Labor in Society*, Durkheim used the word to describe a disturbing phenomenon he observed:

In the middle ages, the worker everywhere lived at the side of his master, pursuing his tasks in the same shop, in the same establishment. Both were part of the same corporation and led the same existence. Hence, conflicts were wholly unusual. Beginning with the fifteenth century, things began to change. The occupational circle is no longer a common organization; it is an exclusive possession of the masters, who alone decide all matters. . . . From that time, a sharp line is drawn between masters and workers. Once this separation was effected, quarrels became numerous. At the same time that specialization becomes greater, revolts become more frequent. The smallest cause for discontent was enough to upset an establishment and cause a worker unhappiness who did not respect the decision of the community.

The Industrial Revolution widened the division between master and worker. The social order fractured ever faster, the bonds of commonality slipped ever looser. By the 20th century, anomy had acquired wider meanings: "a collapse of the social structures governing a given society; the state of alienation experienced by an individual or class in such a situation; personal disorganization resulting in unsocial behavior." In our day anomy has come to mean a social order without norms, without purpose or identity.

In this regard one must question what is a social order? This writer places the business environment within a given corporation high on the social order. That is where adults spend the majority of their time. And for the retail- and service-driven business sector, that is most certainly where behavioral norms are vitally essential. Unfortunately, much of today's emerging workforce is infected with "corporate anomy."

> *In our day anomy has come to mean a social order without norms, without purpose or identity.*

And if this anomy is so prevalent within the workforce (and my professional experience suggests so), there is no wonder that it is compounded by the personal lives of our adult populace. Professor Robert D. Putnam of Harvard, writing in *The American Prospect*, an academic quarterly, points out the decline in membership of voluntary organizations such as the PTA, the League of Women Voters, and the Red Cross in the last thirty years. "Americans today are significantly less engaged with their communities than they were a generation ago," writes Mr. Putnam. A by-product of this decline is a loss of what the scholar calls social trust, or individual faith in others.

Putnam argues that heavy television watching, particularly among the baby boomer generation, pulls people away from group memberships. The more people watch television, the less they read. Other studies have shown a marked falloff in newspaper reading among Generation X, or those born in the last thirty years.

"Heavy readers (of newspapers) are avid joiners, whereas heavy viewers are more likely to be loners," writes Putnam. "Heavy watchers of TV are unusually skeptical about the benevolence of other people." People who rely more on television news than print tend to overestimate crime rates. "Heavy TV watching may well increase pessimism about human nature." Are you at all surprised? Where was that television censorship chip twenty or thirty years ago? It would have helped to some degree, if we would have used it. But, don't lay all the blame on network programming!

It is a philosophical dilemma in that connected can both be and not be at the same time.

Authors Alvin and Heidi Toffler, whose visionary books on social evolution are required reading for serious strategic thinkers, go a step further. They contend that the information age and its potent effect on communication present a dilemma. Through computer connectivity, fiber optic cable TV networks, and satellite links, people have more ways to be interactively in touch than ever in history. Yet we can do it all in complete isolation, void of any physical contact with other humans. It is a philosophical dilemma in that *connected* can both *be* and *not be* at the same time.

Anomy ran like a thread through the go-go '80s. Evidence of the eroding "social trust" was profound. As the decade drew to a close, an economic landscape that once seemed promising was littered with failures wrought by excess — banks toppling like dominoes; a massive government bailout to cover collapsed savings and loans, whose leaders lacked the ethics to keep them as *thrifts*; a HUD scandal that reeled from sweetheart deals to the politically connected, costing taxpayers millions.

So, corporate America (big business and small) is infected with anomy. Perhaps the most striking example of a company enveloped in this corporate phantasmagoria was the Helmsley Hotel empire. In the '80s, when Leona Helmsley stood trial in New York, employees revealed a level of callousness on her part that fueled the tabloids' hunger for a bona fide villain, a living symbol of all that seemed wrong with American business. Let's find a scapegoat. Leona became the poster girl for anti-business crusaders.

As the facts came to light, she seemed to give them plenty of fuel for the bonfire. They publicly moaned about how a lady so rich could be so petty and so consumed with greed. One extreme account found her purportedly firing a chambermaid on the spot — in front of astonished visiting dignitaries — when the worker nervously dropped a tray of pastries and tea.

It was argued by many that Leona Helmsley's treatment of her staff mirrored a cynicism toward her clients. The mission of a hotel, as of any corporation, is to provide good service, thereby ensuring continued patronage. In the '80s, Helmsley Palace's ad agency (Beaver Silverstein) helped push room occupancy from 24 to 87 percent with an image campaign that featured Leona in the hotel, saying: "I wouldn't settle for skimpy towels. Why should you?"

Clever ads masked a more sinister view of the Helmsley domain. Leona Helmsley may not have been skimping on towels for her clientele, but she treated her

> *Leona Helmsley may not have been skimping on towels for her clientele, but she treated her employees as expendable, renewable resources. She failed to recognize the most important element in customer relations: the people who deliver the service.*

employees as expendable, renewable resources. She failed to recognize the most important element in customer relations: the people who deliver the service.

After serving time in prison for evading taxes, Helmsley returned to the hotel with a print campaign that read in part: "Say what you will, she still runs a hell of a hotel." It's a perilous slogan, frivolous at best, arrogant at worst. Many persons reportedly felt avenged when she went to jail. People on her payroll gave incriminating testimony at the trial. For her to trumpet "Say what you will . . ." seemed unnecessarily blithe.

Contrast this situation with the motto of The Ritz-Carlton Hotels: "Ladies and gentlemen serving ladies and gentlemen." This slogan is not just part of a manufactured image; it arises from a social contract. It is truly a part of the identity of the company, and its background is interesting.

THE RITZ-CARLTON TRADITION

THE RITZ-CARLTON®

"Ladies and gentlemen serving ladies and gentlemen."

Ritz-Carlton is one of the world's great hotel chains, not simply because its customers are affluent; care, service, and respect are central to Ritz's internal culture. The executive ranks do not hide themselves behind a desensitized corporate veil making decisions with disregard to the human and emotional component. Upper-echelon managers down to the newest bellhop know the credo of serving the customer.

The hotel budgets a layer of expenses that empowers any employee to cover unexpected needs for guests. Yes, any employee, at the individual's own discretion, is authorized to spend up to $2,000 to correct a problem for a guest. The rationale is simple yet profound: if it takes $150 to retrieve lost baggage or $350 to provide an emergency service, so be it. The investment reaps dividends in the guest who remembers the service and returns again and again to The Ritz-Carlton. Guests pass the word along to their counterparts too. But more importantly, the investment builds huge amounts of emotional equity in the spirit of the employee who was empowered to do it! All layers of the organization, including bellhops and chambermaids, enjoy the privilege of expending hotel resources if necessary to ensure the mission, without fear of a supervisor's dismay for going over budget.

Here is a corporate tradition that takes as much pride in its employees as it does in its clientele and builds on a presumption of integrity. The profit margin reflects the quality of the credo, "Ladies and gentlemen serving ladies and gentlemen."

CHAPTER

2

A MODERN DILEMMA

A MODERN DILEMMA
Reengineering with Honor

One of the many challenges to the leaders of corporate America is how to maintain decency and fair play during the confusion of restructuring. Companies have been decentralized, downsized, spun off, and taken over. Often they are reconfigured without any apparent concrete sense of purpose, other than to eliminate expenses.

Despite their value, technologies accelerate and aggravate change.

A company has begun its disassembly and its future hangs in the balance when those at the top ignore that there are long term implications and ramifications when you lose the spiritual support and understanding of the workforce. Important battles are not won by mercenaries; they are won by patriots. Change may be inevitable, but allowing workers to keep their patriotic honor in the midst of restructuring an organization is not impossible.

Such rending changes cut against our sense of what America means — a land of prosperity for those willing to work hard, save and make reasonable sacrifices to get ahead. Those of us in corporate America keep hearing horror stories of mid-level managers thrown into a free-fall when a company downsizes. What should one think about the stories of laid-off, long-established executives, refused admittance to retrieve personal belongings because the company now fears that their mere presence will cause a disturbance? Losing one's job is humbling, if not traumatic, enough.

Consider the man who held a six-figure position, lost it and ended up driving an airport shuttle bus, only to find the supervisor who fired him stepping on board. Is it also no wonder that anomy is bred within an organization when such stories are discussed within the corporate grapevine?

The Rev. William J. Byron, a Jesuit priest and distinguished professor of management at Georgetown University, has studied this disquieting phenomenon with a unique focus. His book, *Finding Work Without Losing Heart*, taps a wide interview base in advising those who once held high-level jobs and find themselves seeking work in the rough seas of a shifting economy and business environment.

"Managers in America," writes Father Byron, "are living in a new corporate world. At the very top, they are less secure, although they are much more generously compensated. At lower levels, managerial men and women are less inclined to rely on the corporation for their security, more inclined toward entrepreneurial behavior within the corporation (as are partisan politicians within Congress), and always open to new opportunities to match their developing assemblage of managerial skills. This is a new entrepreneurial age within well-established corporations." Byron quotes the advice given to CEOs by Jim Herget, managing director of Kern/ Ferry, an executive search firm in Cleveland, "Be flexible around an inflexible set of core values — God, family, country, job."

Byron continues:

> Persons looking for security and long-term satisfaction in the corporate world will often be disappointed, said Herget; the organization of the future will be "smaller, with more rolling, contingent relationships." He reminded me that today's young adults

are more hesitant and cynical in approaching the corporation because of what they have seen happen on the news, in their cities, and to their fathers. This explains much of their interest in benefit negotiations, a matter often taken for granted in days gone by.

Is this our future? Paucity of long-term employment, smaller organizations with rolling relationships, hesitant youth, and executives bedeviled by instability? It is not so indelibly written. Just as politicians, churches and schools focus on values on the homefront, wise business leaders can pursue manifesting the bonds and productive aspects of the culture of yesteryear. It is being very profitably achieved by many of our leading business success stories, and I will quantify how and why it should be emulated elsewhere.

THE CULTURAL CRUSADE

To start a corporate cultural crusade, one must first and foremost be realistic. Top executives are driven by profit factors. Companies will give values or culture only lip service if there are no profits to be had and only expenses to be incurred.

Technologies accelerate and aggravate change. Television feeds us instantaneous news which is viewed raw, without the leavening of time and reflection. Satellite communication and computer networks bring us a mass of data, albeit frequently person to person, but often without a frame of cultural reference between sender and receiver. We are living in the decades-old Toffler scenario: *Future Shock*.

Since we are not going to retreat technologically, we must use the benefits of technology *pro-actively* for the business's cultural benefit. We must remember that artists in every age have warned that no man is an island. Even if a company is not in the midst of downsizing, when its workforce is habitually left out of the loop, uninformed, or excluded from the company's latest news, workers are being unintentionally influenced — the debilitating message of *isolation* is sent. Technology, closed circuit television, and computer networking pose opportunities as well as problems.

FedEx is noted as having one of the world's most technologically effective, complex and geographically dispersed logistics and delivery systems. They have achieved this in the midst of maintaining a highly spirited and dedicated employee service culture.

Fred Smith, Federal Express founder, is outspoken on the topic of creating the essential bond between employee emotion and company mission.

On a busy day, the FedEx hub at Memphis will process more than 1,000,000 packages to their guaranteed overnight delivery points. With several hundred thousand employees navigating FedEx's international air and roadways, communication on a multitude of fronts is nonnegotiable. Effective communication simply has to occur each time — every time — in a myriad of languages, local dialects, and distant delivery points.

Fred Smith, FedEx founder, is outspoken on the topic of creating the *essential* bond between employee emotion and company mission.

The FedEx service mission is to treat every customer's package as their most important package and to deliver it on time. The company aggressively pursues making each employee feel like a stakeholder in the process. Employees are not just kept in the loop on the company's development and activities — they are actually talked to, directly, every morning for up to ninety minutes by a constantly rotating cast of corporate leaders. FedEx has created its own satellite television network and downlinks its reception

to literally thousands of offices worldwide. Every day *FedEx T.V.* features employee profiles, delivery news updates, phone-in "Question and Answer" opportunities (a la Larry King), and competitive information, etc. You name it, *FedEx T.V.* will focus on it to keep the culture vibrant and its employees feeling connected. The environment today, perhaps more than ever before, requires that we guard against a corporate mentality that sees people as expendable items in an ever-spiraling quest for profits.

But you don't need billions of dollars of revenue flow and hundreds of thousands of employees to afford letting modern technology enhance your culture and service achievements. Station Casinos — Midwest Division — has strategically planned a systematic, vertically-integrated initiative that is based on the principles and disciplines of internal marketing — corporate culture, training, communication, motivation, and measurement. It draws thematic cohesion from "The Eye of the Tiger," the casino's vision statement signature. At the core of this system is the Station Casinos Midwest version of the FedEx TV.

At some point the corporation must acknowledge that its essence is people, that people make the profits, and people need to feel part of the loop; human nature craves to belong.

When launched later this year, "TVTV" (Tiger Vision Television) will feed closed-circuit news broadcasts to television monitors carefully positioned in areas throughout the property where employees congregate or pass regularly — break rooms, employee dining room, employee entrance, and the like. TVTV is produced, directed, and anchored by Tiger Team members (Tiger Team is the collective term for Station Casino St. Charles employees), who also serve as the editorial board. They use in-house facilities, set up at surprisingly minimal expense. They are trained and mentored by professional strategic video producers to ensure that the content of the news program stays on target and is effectively presented.

The format is simple and straightforward. It is supplemented periodically by professionally-produced video "packages" for added impact and interest. The subject matter is focused on strategic and corporate culture issues: tactical and operational news, anticipated impact of upcoming events, competitive activity and related business information, personnel changes, employee rewards and promotions, and cultural stories and reinforcement features.

Technology need not be the nemesis of the corporate quest. It has been strategically managed to play a valuable role in many organizational service cultures. On the exterior, many companies that succeed in being very "soft touch" in their behavior, have a behind the scenes complement that is quite "hi-tech."

At some point, however, to actually achieve this state of consciousness, the corporation must acknowledge that its essence is people, that people make the profits, and that one must safeguard an awareness of our common cause in the human enterprise. People need to feel part of the loop; human nature craves to *belong*.

CHAPTER

3

THE SURROGATE TRIBE

THE SURROGATE TRIBE
The Role of Corporations

Emile Durkheim postulated that, for the worker, the corporation took the place in social relations of the ancient blood tribe. The cultural influence of the corporation, he held, became an analog for the tribal customs of old. Modern studies in ethnology, psychology and religion establish that the mind of man is tamed and nourished by symbols and stories and heroic examples; these provide the path to self-identification. Durkheim helps preface my argument that the corporation has an influence as a social force, as well as a responsibility as a business entity.

> *Durkheim postulated that, for the worker, the corporation took the place in social relations of the ancient blood tribe. The cultural influence of the corporation, he held, became an analog for the tribal customs of old.*

Heroes can be built and myths can be woven. One of anthropologist Joseph Campbell's key insights was that a myth within a society does not have to be true to be relevant and to persevere. Essentially, it becomes a myth simply because of its sustenance. In its transcendence from generation to generation, it assumes more meaning. A valued myth will enlarge with time.

A myth is not restricted only to tribes, religions or society. Myths live within the society of business. Durkheim was prescient in noting that our corporations have in many ways become society for their employees whose beliefs and value structures are significantly impacted by their surroundings. And, today, most people spend the majority of their waking hours in the surroundings of the workplace — replete with its rumors, legends, ceremonies, and myths.

We must, as a society, recognize that the *corporation*, however, is purely a large tribe of people. It is man who has the responsibility to men. There can be no corporate veil — management must connect with supervisors, and as well as with the line-level employees. CEOs and corporate board members cannot use the insulation of their positions to shield themselves from the human impact — both positive and negative — of their corporate actions. The most temporal element that determines an organization's destiny is man, not matter.

> *We must, as a society, recognize that the corporation, however, is purely a large tribe of people.*

Studies by Joseph Campbell further underscore the essential place for heroes, myths and legends in maintaining the tribal culture. According to Campbell, tribalism is the glue that binds the social order together. It is no less prevalent today than in antiquity, although the display of tribal behavior is more circumspect and less obvious.

Durkheim felt that in the nineteenth century the workplace had emerged as the dominant tribal influence in modern life. It still is today. Corporate management can profit from understanding the dynamics of tribal ritual. It is these unspectacular ceremonies carried out in offices, restaurants and other workplaces every day that pull employees together in meaningful, shared experience.

Ritual symbolizes and memorializes tribal myths and legends, "acting out" the lessons of a culture and the customs which dictate the rules of conduct within the group. Rituals bind members of a group together.

Tampering with ritual can have profound

consequences. When new management in a company —
with the stroke of pen — demolishes cherished rituals,
the results can be very different from the expectation. The
annual company picnic, the monthly company
performance review breakfast, or the interdepartmental
Halloween decorating contest may seem like superfluous
indulgences to a budget-cutting bean-counter. To the
employees, however, it could be the only real emotional
link they have to the company, to other departments, and
to the legacy of the company's culture. The manager who
is cavalier in dismissing the rituals of the tribe not only
becomes the despoiler of its heritage, but a potential
enemy of the tribe itself. Management can't be blind to
the human component. Management is people, and so
are the line-level employees.

The sensible manager sees the value of rituals which
promulgate the desired culture and perpetuates them as
prized assets. And an executive who is astute in rooting
out traditions that are detrimental to the culture should
replace them with activities that convey appropriate
behavioral lessons.

Building strong corporate cultures will not heal all
of society's ills. But the companies that strive to do so
will have a decided advantage over those that don't. The
effort will also be one step in re-establishing social stability
in America. It won't replace the need for school, church,
government, and especially family to focus on rebuilding
values. But it makes good business and social sense.

So the question becomes — how does one build a
strong, positive corporate culture?

CHAPTER

4

THE HUNT FOR LOST BASICS

THE HUNT FOR LOST BASICS
Reigniting the Fire

In searching for answers on how to build or reinforce a corporate culture, organizations often want to go *back to the basics* without realizing what the basics are. The basics are surely different from what they once were. Technologies have changed. Processes have changed. What employees found acceptable yesterday may be grounds for a lawsuit today. What investors expected at one time may be quite remote compared to their demands today.

For many organizations, the *basics* are felt to be the things that worked when a company was in its heady entrepreneurial mode. In the early days of a company's evolution, there is often a pioneering spirit, a sense of excitement and adventure, and a strong camaraderie among the staff. Managers roll up their sleeves and pitch in with hourly employees, working into the night to get the job done on time. There's pride and dedication to a cause. The organization may be relatively small, with a strong sense of family. Decisions can be made quickly, often based on instinct and intuition rather than laborious research data or endless committee meetings. It is a time of taking risks, sometimes all-or-nothing risks that can make or break the company. Operational systems are fairly informal and are frequently

> *In the early days of a company's evolution, there is often a pioneering spirit, a sense of excitement and adventure, and a strong camaraderie among the staff.*

altered. Ad hoc procedures often pop up to deal with particular situations and then fade away when the situation is past. A take-no-prisoners, damn-the-torpedoes, full-speed-ahead operating style is not uncommon. The basics of this time in a company's life are straight out of Horatio Alger — work hard, work fast, work steady, and success will follow.

For those companies that get past the survival stage, growth and maturity bring a new set of challenges. With growth, companies typically evolve into bureaucracies. Organizations become departmentalized, decentralized and desensitized. Communication and connectivity within the organization begin to dry up. Thousands of memos that are supposed to communicate become misunderstood or simply go unread — too much volume and too little clarity. A lot of paper or e-mail circulates, but information and ideas do not.

> *Organizations become departmentalized, decentralized and desensitized. A lot of paper or e-mail circulates, but information and ideas do not.*

In ensuing generations, a company's new leadership has less understanding of what was anchoring the corporate culture, how it should be maintained, and how to manifest a culture in the current organization. At this point, corporate anomy can grow exponentially. Values get buried under operational matters or profit objectives. The fervor that drove the entrepreneurial stage of a company becomes muddled; momentum slows; inertia sets in. It then becomes difficult, if not impossible, to mobilize for new challenges or crises in the marketplace.

Bureaucracies typically reward mediocrity. (Try to get a document at City Hall.) *Bureauthink* snuffs out initiative by individual employees (who may have better ideas than the group) and, in its extreme form, is incapable of producing any innovative solutions to problems. That is why *reorganizations* can so easily accommodate de-layering and layoffs. The worker or manager who plods along and never makes waves or attempts innovation can have a comfortable existence, or so it would appear until the shock waves of downsizing — euphemistically called *right sizing* — sweep through a company and wipe out those comfortable existences. A company with large numbers of time-nurtured redundancies becomes barren of imagination and vision and devoid of passion. (Remove 20% of City Hall's workers and your service product will either be the same or amazingly improved. You may in fact get faster, friendlier service because someone cares — and is *involved*. *Bureaucracies* are all around us, not just in government.)

BASICS THAT REALLY COUNT

The most essential basics transcend all other details. They can be counted on one hand. To wit:

> *Passion is vital to a corporate culture — passion for the values of the organization, passion for what the group stands for.*

PASSION: Passion is vital to a corporate culture — passion for the values of the organization, passion for what the group stands for. Fed Ex has passion. Nordstrom has passion. Walt Disney World has it too. The passion is manifested in the loyalty of the employees, knowledge of and dedication to the company's ideals, and the pride that shows in a worker's face. An excellent example of passion transcending organizational levels exists at Southwest Airlines. Their no-frills flights are more than a way for price conscious consumers to travel from point A to point B; the flights are an airborne stage. From the time the ticket agent in shorts and polo shirt calls for boarding, which is first come first served, to the time one disembarks, something magical happens. CEOs sit next to college students who

sit next to housewives. Everyone can have a relaxing and entertaining time because the employees of Southwest make it possible. They are able to make it possible because Herb Kelleher, CEO, has passion. If a flight attendant sings "I left my heart in San Francisco" over the intercom upon landing in California it is not because he is paid to; it is because he accepts and embraces the corporate culture, the organization's values, and what the organization stands for. As one Southwest passenger put it, "Southwest Airlines is like a mini Mardi Gras." The loyalty and dedication to one's company above and beyond the call of duty is often referred to as *Organizational Citizenship Theory*. Obviously, Southwest has a motivated, entertaining group of citizens.

> *Wholehearted, unqualified, recognizable zeal from the leaders at the very top is not just important, it is absolutely required for a strong culture to flourish.*

COMMITMENT FROM THE TOP: Wholehearted, unqualified, *recognizable zeal* from the leaders at the very top is not just important, it is absolutely required for a strong culture to flourish. Lee Iacocca had commitment at Chrysler, and everyone knew it. During his reign, the message came down to the rank and file. There was no doubt in anyone's mind as Chrysler was rebuilt nearly from ashes. Today, they compete proudly among the world's major automakers — largely because of Iacocca's rejuvenating vision and mission. Yes, luck, timing, and government assistance played a part; but without the retooling push and entrepreneurial culture led by Iacocca, there would likely be no Chrysler today.

CHRYSLER ® **FOLLOW-THROUGH:** Delivering on promises — to customers, vendors, and employees — is the proof of commitment, the tangible evidence that management means what it says.

Don Hill, a retired marketing executive from Texaco, was noted by many within his company for his admiration of the Nordstrom company and its commitment to service. He frequently passed along a legendary story to new marketing representatives about a Nordstrom sales clerk who cheerfully accepted the return of a malfunctioning, one-year-old, used chain saw.

The cooperative attitude of the sales clerk was not the focus of the story, nor was the age of the chain saw. The climatic point of the story occurs when the next person in line observed to the Nordstrom clerk that she didn't realize the company even sold chain saws. The clerk's response: "We don't, but our mission is to exceed our customers expectations, and that gentleman means everything to the future of my company."

The legacy of service, cooperation and consistency within the Nordstrom ranks is widely heralded.

A personal experience revolves around a time I was trying to get Mr. Bill Nordstrom, co-president of Nordstrom on the telephone. The secretary in the Seattle headquarters said he was not in, but she believed she could locate him. After less than a minute of holding, and then two rings of the phone, Mr. Nordstrom was on the line. She had gotten through to him at the first floor, cosmetics section of a Nordstrom's in Chicago! Best yet, he wasn't expecting my call, nor did he know why I was calling.

Consistency in applying policies and procedures - for all ranks and across all departmental lines - is the evidence of fairness and justice.

Not only does this illustrate passion and commitment from the top, but it goes beyond traditional follow-through and the effective use of technology. Nordstrom has its *cultural dominoes* quite in order, and as long as visionaries are at the helm, don't expect a single one of them to topple, irrespective of a bad fiscal quarter now and then. This vision reaches much farther out than three months or a year.

CONSISTENCY: Consistency in applying policies and procedures — for all ranks and across all departmental lines — is the evidence of fairness and justice. It keeps effective human and interpersonal communications on the same foundation.

RESPECT: Respect for employees, for suppliers, and, above all, for customers separates the *class* companies from the followers. But almost invariably, the most esteemed companies, those appearing on various lists of commendation, exhibit an environment of respect. Respect is an ideal that is easy to *talk* but hard to *walk*.

> *Respect for employees, for suppliers, and, above all, for customers separates the class companies from the followers. Respect is an ideal that is easy to talk but hard to walk.*

A MATTER OF SPIRIT

Going back to basics is not about proficiencies, regimens in operation, or training. It is about spirit. It is a simple pride in doing a job right all the time. It's about rekindling a Cal Ripken, Jr. mentality in employees, management and other stakeholders. When Ripken, the Baltimore Orioles shortstop, broke Lou Gehrig's record for consecutive games played — a record once thought impossible to beat — he said, "I don't know what all the fuss is about. I'm just doing my job." Just doing his job for 2,131 straight games and then some.

BEN & JERRY'S HOMEMADE BASIC VALUES

One company to note that has made values virtually synonymous with its corporate mission is Ben & Jerry's Homemade, Inc., makers of premium ice cream, frozen yogurt, and ice cream novelties. Founded in 1978 by childhood friends Ben Cohen and Jerry Greenfield, the Vermont-based company markets its products through supermarkets, grocery stores, convenience stores, and food service operations nationwide. Hundreds of Ben & Jerry's franchised scoop shops do business in a couple dozen states. The company, which was launched on $12,000 (a third of which was borrowed), generated a $5.95 million profit in 1995.

In 1988 the company created a Statement of Mission, dedicated to "a new corporate concept of linked prosperity," according to its literature. "Our mission consists of three interrelated parts: product, economic, and social."

The Product Mission: "To make, distribute, and sell the finest quality, all natural ice cream and related products in a wide variety of innovative flavors made from Vermont dairy products."

The Economic Mission: "To operate the Company on a sound financial basis of profitable growth, increasing value for our shareholders, and creating career opportunities and financial rewards for our employees."

The Social Mission: "To operate the Company in a way that actively recognizes the central role that business plays in the structure of society by initiating innovative trends to improve the quality of a broad community — local, national, and international . . . while

(Continued on next page)

BEN & JERRY'S BASIC VALUES

(Continued from previous page)

holding a deep respect for individuals, inside and outside the company, and for communities of which they are a part."

Ben & Jerry's gives away 7.5 percent of its pre-tax earnings through a company foundation. It also has employee Community Action Teams at five Vermont sites. And, it makes corporate grants through the Director of Social Mission Developments. "The Foundation is managed by a nine member employee board and considers proposals relating to children and families, disenfranchised groups, and the environment."

In a candid 1994 message from the founders, accompanying the annual report, Ben and Jerry assessed the need to streamline (and expand) production facilities, and discussed the selection of the new CEO, Bob Holland. Some people, they observed, viewed the company's difficulties as partly "a result of our efforts to redefine the relationship between business and the community, in short, that 'this social responsibility stuff only goes so far.'

"Quite the contrary. We are as committed to this vision as we have ever been. To be sure, we must bring greater business discipline to this task. But we have built a strong company on this vision. It is the combination of this vision and better discipline that will keep us strong and growing."

Vision. Discipline. Strength. Buzzwords one hears at motivational seminars and at banquets with the best inspirational speakers. Yet here is a company with more than 350 headquarters employees which has linked those words and bonded its corporate emotions and ethics not only with its employees, but with the surrounding community.

CHAPTER

VISION, VALUES AND MISSION

VISION, VALUES & MISSION

Clarity is Essential

A company without vision is like a blindfolded javelin thrower. Without a way to aim and get a good run toward the target, who knows what damage might be done, let alone what will be hit? A given company can be reasonably successful if its movements are confined to a small area where the obstacles are well known. Both large and small companies alike are proving that operating outside one's comfort zone can be awkward and halting, and can create vulnerability to the predations of others who have a clear sight of the terrain. Visionless companies will ultimately experience serious damage.

The vision of a company lies in its destination, what it seeks to achieve and, equally important, what it wants to be. How a company identifies itself as a corporate citizen is crucial to building a solid vision statement. The vision is like a compass, guiding a firm not just toward profits, but on a voyage of self-definition. Such a vision drives performance and gives direction to decision making. It focuses the organization on a target and bonds the people together in a common quest. There is an aura of purpose in a company with a view of where it is going. But it is astounding how few companies truly have a vision. What passes for a vision in most companies is a financial projection or how many new locations it plans to open. Too infrequently does one find an upper level executive in corporate America who displays real vision; and, in a typical company, rarely do middle or lower level managers demonstrate signs of visionary understanding (which can stem from lack of vision or fear of speaking candidly in a constrained environment).

By and large, the vision of American CEOs has become constrained by the stock market or The Board which holds the Damoclean sword above each of them. Capitalism, the dynamic engine of the most powerful nation in the history of the world, is being sacrificed for get-rich-faster or stay-rich myopia. Not many top managers take a politically unpopular stand or are willing to hold back profits today to invest in a motivational or cultural expansion concept that should help enhance the future. Unfortunately, that is because most management today does not have a clear focus on what the future is and where such an investment should be directed.

"If you don't know where you're going, you'll probably end up some place else."

— Yogi Berra

In the inimitable words of baseball legend Yogi Berra, "If you don't know where you're going, you'll probably end up some place else." The absence of a clear vision for a company and a solid sense of destination leaves the ship rudderless and adrift, carried by tide and wind in whatever direction the elements pitch.

To be sure, many companies proclaim a vision or a mission statement. Too often these statements are convoluted or meaningless to all but a few, and no more than a self-important comment about a "commitment to excellence" or "ultimate quality."

These statements are good for the egos of the top executives and look good, they think, on the plaque in the foyer. They are also handy during media interviews, or for opening speeches at annual conventions. Yet, when asked, seldom can anyone in the company repeat the vision and mission of the company, even in an employee's own words, let alone verbatim. The reason is that those same words that give such comfort to corporate leadership are lost on most in the company who don't understand or don't care about those words — *the words don't connect with them!*

One frequent problem with vision and mission statements is that they are created by committees. Committees inherently try to cover all the bases and include everybody's viewpoint so nobody feels left out. Political bureaus tend to manage or dictate — but not lead! That's why the statements are often cumbersome, nebulous or generic. At International Marketing Systems, we've even encountered an organization with several visions, innumerable *corporate* missions by departments, and heaven knows how much uncertainty in the ranks.

The clarity of Walt Disney's vision was singular - "We create happiness ." He understood that he was not building a place but an experience. Today, the Disneyland vision resonates around the globe.

Most successful vision statements generally derive from the view of perceptive leaders who can prognosticate what the future should involve. The clarity of Walt Disney's vision was singular. He persevered with his vision even, at times, over the objections of his associates (including his own brother). He understood that he was not building "Disney Land" a place but *Disneyland the experience.* Thus Walt Disney's Disneyland vision — *We create happiness* — resonates in Disney properties around the globe.

For James C. Collins, author of *Built to Last*, the successful vision must be about building clocks, not telling time. Writes Collins: "Having a great idea or being a charismatic leader is 'time telling'; building a company that can prosper far beyond the tenure of any single leader and through multiple product life cycles is 'clock building.' Those who build visionary companies tend to be clock builders. Their primary accomplishment is not the implementation of a great idea, the expression of a charismatic personality, or the accumulation of wealth. It is the company itself and what it stands for."

Mac Hadden, the president of a large regional industrial supply distributorship once said, "I want a mission statement that the pickers in the warehouse can understand and quote." He understood and wanted the power of simplicity, the clarity of a single-minded focused vision (and mission) that everyone in the organization can share and support. Every Marine recruit quickly learns what *Semper Fidelis* means, the commitment of the Corps to be "always faithful" to country and comrade. At East Jefferson Hospital, a large health care center in the New Orleans metropolitan area, even the housekeepers can recite the hospital's simple service mission, "Providing Care and Comfort: Our Highest Mission." And at Touro, one of New Orleans' most venerable health care suppliers, they seem to have gone one step farther with their simple yet penetrating service mission: "We treat everyone like family."

A mission statement should be focused, memorable, and possible. A vision and its correlated mission should distill the organization's values. These terms, vision and mission, are often used interchangeably in corporate conversations. In my view they are separate but related. The vision is the destination: the mission is how to get

> *A mission statement should be focused, memorable and possible. The vision is the destination: the mission is how to get there. All too often, companies have a mission statement (how) without a guiding vision (what or where).*

there. All too often, companies have a mission statement (how) without a guiding vision (what, where, or why). As the captain said to his passengers: "The good news is, we're making great time. The bad news is, we've been going in circles for hours."

CORPORATE VALUES

The values of an organization define its character, the way it looks at itself, its world, and its interaction with that world. Values determine how a company treats its employees, its suppliers, and the community around it. If it operates by sturdy and honorable values, it is probably a good corporate citizen. If it does not, chances are it is embroiled in controversy — or heading toward it. For companies like these, there always seem to be problems: personnel difficulties, like high turnover; disputes with community members; or strained relations with vendors. In America most corporations probably fall midscale between value extremes. Responsible executives do not ignore the impact that self-indulgence or corner-cutting and cold personnel decisions have upon the broader consciousness of their ranks.

There is much talk nationally about erosion of *family values* in American society. Yet, as Durkheim noted as early as 1896, little is said about *corporate values* in the same context. It remains true a century later. This could either reflect a very high regard for business and a belief that the values are in place or it could bespeak a cynicism so deep that the prospect of finding values in business seems a contradiction in terms.

Of course there are exceptions, companies who speak frankly of their values, like Empress Casino, a riverboat operation in the Midwest. It has adopted its own sense of values, a *footprint* based on integrity, respect, and caring. While one could argue the irony of the gaming industry (which is frequently attacked as a detriment to social values) promoting values — I argue that this is

> *Paradigm analysis examines the current state of an organization, identifying the key issues of the status quo — what makes the company tick.*

welcome. Like it or not, gaming has evolved, entering the competitive mainstream of entertainment, replete with restaurants, hotels, celebrity acts, and more. The element of chance at these casino resorts does not obviate the fact that thousands of hard-working Americans are employed in casino resorts. Corporate values must ultimately resonate in the vision and emotion of the individual — not in an inaccessible corporation. In the case of Empress, the drive behind the force of their footprint was that of former president Kevin Larson, who had the conviction and commitment to *walk the walk* of promoting values in their workplace. . . . More and more Kevin Larsons should and likely will be taking the helms of service vessels.

STRATEGIES FOR A VALUES-BASED CULTURE

At International Marketing Systems we work with clients in a process that helps focus on the organization's values. The process builds on a company's cultural strengths and its progressively developing personality. We adhere to three strategic steps in directing the development of a values-based culture (IMS refers to this process as, "Internal Marketing"):

> *Strategic planning for internal marketing addresses the cultural issues of an organization.*

- *Paradigm analysis*
- *Strategic planning for internal marketing*
- *Mobilization*

A paradigm analysis examines the current state of an organization, identifying the key issues of the status quo — what makes the company tick.

Strategic planning for internal marketing (different from, but a valuable girder for, financial projection strategies or business and marketing planning) addresses with priority focus the cultural issues of an organization, that is, the aspect of the paradigm that prompts a company to act on its ideals. Mobilization is the requisite follow-through. Without implementation and execution, the analysis and planning are but a waste of time and resources. Worse, lack of action after stirring interest in an initiative serves notice to the employees that management has no commitment to the process. Morale and confidence in the company diminish.

> *Mobilization is the requisite follow-through. Without implementation and execution, the analysis and planning are but a waste of time and resources.*

Internal marketing, however, is similar to external marketing. Communications are intended to influence the behavior of the company's audience (i.e., its employees and other closely related stakeholders). External marketing (advertising, promotions, etc.) seeks to reach consumers with the company's message and to influence their behavior, thereby turning consumers into customers. Internal marketing does the same, but with employees. It is the road map for activities to shape the culture of the company.

Building a culture with the desired attributes requires consistency, determination and discipline. In other words, you have to keep at it to make it work. That's the way with advertising too. Even after a level has been reached which signals that the values have taken hold, it is imperative to keep the values top-of-mind, freshen up the concepts periodically, and reward those who manifest the ethos. What CEO stops his ongoing advertising campaign because sales are okay? Does it make sense to stop internal marketing because customer satisfaction and the corporate culture are in O.K. shape? When advertising stops, sales coast and ultimately slip. When internal marketing stops, the culture of a company can be expected to slip.

CHAPTER

CHANGE: FORCE FOR GOOD OR ILL?

CHANGE
Force for Good or Ill?

There are pundits now who predict a world of chaotic and constant change. Some say this is to be desired, that change is dynamic and prevents a company from becoming stale. "If it's not broken, change it!" Change, however, is not always for the better and change for the sake of change can be meaningless and counterproductive. At the same time, arbitrary resistance to change is futile. A certain degree of change is inevitable in the modern marketplace; yet, in today's environment, a company that is rooted in firm, immutable values is far better set to deal with technological or systemic change than one that is not. A popular country-and-western song says, "If you don't stand for something, you'll fall for anything." Putting values at the core of a corporate culture strengthens the operational standards; in most cases, under careful management, whatever may seem to be a sacrifice in short-term profits will pay greater dividends in the long term. A company is only as good as the sum of its workers.

VIRTUOUS ACTION
Values become virtues when they are turned into action. Values must become so much a part of a body that acting on them comes naturally and spontaneously, without conscious effort. When a company's values become completely ingrained into its culture — become its culture — so that they intimately guide the actions of the

management and employees, that company should be called *virtuous*. And, when a company has a virtuous culture, it can probably sustain all the reorganization and change management can dole out. This is because change is typically an organizational phenomenon not a cultural phenomenon.

> *The state of virtue is the ultimate accomplishment for a company with a clear vision and strong values. Companion to its ethical superiority is its strategic advantage in having a sturdy framework of ideals to withstand competitive pressures or changes that increasingly ravage the fabric of business today.*

The state of virtue is the ultimate accomplishment for a company with a clear vision and strong values. Companion to its ethical strength is its strategic advantage in having a sturdy framework of ideals to withstand competitive pressures or changes that increasingly ravage the fabric of business today.

For a company to become virtuous, its members must act on its values. Employees must know and believe in the values. They must have the desire and wherewithal to act accordingly.

CULTURAL ALCHEMY: A METHOD TO THE MAGIC

Advertising maven Howard "Luck" Gossage writes in his book, *Is There Any Hope for Advertising?*, of "capturing magic in a bottle." It is the goal of advertising to create in the consumer's mind a sense that there is a magical quality to the product or service being touted. A deodorant is not a chemical solution to stop perspiration; it is a ticket to love, power, social acceptance, and freedom from anxiety. The *magic* in the bottle may be a supernormal potion (product) or a genie (service) that will obediently fulfill any command.

In advertising, alchemy lies in the magic of the image.

On the other hand, the reality of how it is created is purely pragmatic. Successful, long-lasting companies carefully and strategically construct their products and services. Gossage proclaims that this pragmatic factor is at the root of the company's identity. "Image is surface. Identity is mass." A company should be tending to its identity (mass) long before (and long after) an advertising agency starts luring consumers to its products or services by orchestrating its imagery. Both image and identity require a respective strategic plan.

As with a company's image, a corporate culture should not happen by accident. The corporate ethos must be nurtured. An organization must work constantly to preserve and strengthen its identity just as advertising people work on image. The internal process should be a continuum of activities in a stream of positive reinforcement. Some of the same strategy used in external marketing — the magic in the bottle — should help build the character and personality of the company among its employees.

> *The corporate ethos must be nurtured. An organization must work constantly to preserve and strengthen its identity just as advertising people work on image.*

Inculcating in employees a values-based corporate culture requires a disciplined method. It begins with the first interview when a prospect applies for a job. It should extend through this *hiring* process and continue thereafter with regular intervals of activity to renew interest, reinforce core lessons, and stimulate internalization of desired values. The method must teach the desired norms by example, by actually practicing behavior which meets approved standards. It must be perpetual. Values must become entwined in the warp and woof of the company's cultural fabric at all points so that its own pattern emerges as distinctive and identifiable as a Scot's tartan.

At Walt Disney World, for example, keeping the

DISNEY MISSION REFLECTS TRADITION

Disney World is a prime example of a corporate culture whose mission reflects its tradition. Years ago when Walt Disney was overseeing the construction of Disneyland in Anaheim, cost overruns became an issue. Disney was overextended; his investors were worried; pressure was building. Story has it that a contractor approached Disney with an idea for reducing expenses. The man pointed to the turrets high above on Cinderella's Castle, and said that the stained glass windows could be fabricated with a new style of plastic molding at a substantial savings. Disney said no, reasoning that "I would know that they were fake and we had cheated. Over time *cast members* (Disney employees) working for us would know it and sooner or later a slide-by mentality would rub off on the guests."

Go to 90% of corporate America and ask vice-presidents what their company's mission statement is and most can't answer. Why? It probably doesn't mean that much to them.

grounds spotless is such an integral part of the corporate psyche that it would not at all be considered out of character for chairman Michael Eisner, touring a Disney property with visiting corporate dignitaries, to reach down, pick up a piece of trash and deposit it in the nearest waste bin. It would be as natural for him as closing a million-dollar deal. It is simply part of the DNA of the Disney service culture.

In the folklore of American corporations, Walt Disney World has an almost legendary reputation for appreciation of tradition and employees' commitment to their mission and attention to detail. Stroll down Main Street USA at the sprawling Orlando facility and ask any worker the Disney World mission statement. The answer is immediate: "We create happiness for people of all ages throughout the world." Go to 90 percent of corporate

America and ask vice-presidents what their company's mission statement is and most can't answer. Why? It probably doesn't mean that much to them.

By Disney's logic, a great amusement park ride in a mediocre guest environment won't be as successful as an average ride in a superior guest relations environment like Disney World. Of course Disney doesn't produce mediocre attractions, but the point is not lost on the repeat crowds. People know caring performance when they experience it.

Employees don't just work for Disney. They are "cast for a role" — an extension of the cinematic heritage of the corporation and its founder. Whether the job is sweeping streets or operating an attraction, cast members are motivated to be part of the entertainment; they're not simply encouraged. No, folks aren't told: "You're just as important in your role of turnstile keeper as if you were up there singing on the stage. Don't forget that. Now go out there and be happy, friendly and smile!" Instead, *from the onset*, prospective employees are immersed in the culture — at the first job interview learning of Disney's scrupulous standards that are not meant for all. Those who make it through a sensitive *peer* screening and hiring process then begin to absorb values of the Disney mindset. As new cast members go through a day-long orientation program called *Traditions*, they begin to follow suit. The employees' first exposure to working at Disney World is to the culture — not the function.

> *The employees' first exposure to working at Disney World is to the culture — not the function.*

"Pixie dust" is the metaphor within the corporation that signifies the magic that makes things work at Disney. Put another way, pixie dust is *attention to detail* — something that all corporations hope to achieve. (Note the turret next time you're there and ask a cast member their mission.)

As was illustrated with Ritz-Carlton, and now at Walt

Disney World, cast members must learn and "internalize" that guests do not come simply to enrich the enterprise. Patrons come to be entertained and to leave their problems behind. Cast members learn to treat customers as they would guests in their own homes. They internalize this philosophy through methods, systems, orientation, workshops, and legacy. If a visitor at Disney World looks lost, it's not unusual for a cast member to approach the visitor and say, "Where would you like to go? Follow me and I'll see that you get there." You know you're a guest because the employee makes sure you feel that way.

CHAPTER

STORYTELLING:
WORKING IN THE VINEYARD

STORYTELLING
Working in the Vineyard

Storytelling can be a combustion chamber for one's organization. Great corporations generate a folklore, an internal set of stories that employees absorb like the oral tradition of a family. Tales of the corporate culture can be uplifting or disturbing. They inspire trust and loyalty among employees or leave shards of fear and disenchantment. Stories help build legends and legacy. They can become mythologized.

An oft-told tale in the Disney folklore sends a sharp message to trainees. A young girl visiting Disney World with her aunt (a Disney employee) was dying to meet Snow White; she had a bright red bow ribbon tied in her dark shoulder-length hair and a notebook for Snow White's autograph. A parade of Disney characters passed through the Magic Kingdom. The child and her aunt asked a hostess to help them find Snow White. They got to see Pinocchio and Mickey Mouse, but somehow Snow White was elusive. The hostess, wanting to please her co-worker's niece, decided to break the company rule and take the child just a few steps backstage (behind the scenes) after the parade. Lo, twenty feet away stood Snow White with her back to the family and the hostess. The little girl recognized her by the flowing red cape draped from her

Great corporations generate a folklore, an internal set of stories that employees absorb like the oral tradition of a family.

shoulders and her black hair tied back with a bright red bow ribbon (just like her adoring fan). "Oh, Snow White!" squealed the little girl. Snow White, in all her radiance, turned around — with coffee in hand and a cigarette between her lips. Snow White was on break.

Imagine the blow to a child when the cast member has fallen out of character. As a business school case study one could debate who made the mistake: the hostess, for taking a family back stage, or Snow White, for the cigarette while still in costume.

After the emotional jolt of the story, Disney trainees are quickly told the story is not true. Invariably, some fidgety chuckles come from the roomful of new employees. But the impact of the story proves invaluable. It has turned to myth.

Myths help build a culture and complement the vision.

The apocryphal anecdote permeates Disney folklore. Anyone who goes through Disney University, the training center (and custodian of Disney World's Corporate Culture), understands it as an allegory of the cast-member philosophy, to motivate one to live up to Disney standards and not let any part of the company's culture and heritage down.

Myths, after all, help build a culture and complement the vision. It has been this way as far back as Joseph Campbell's anthropological studies go and it will be so hereafter.

Disney University uses storytelling to fuel the *grapevine* with corporate parables that illustrate desired lessons. The stories are not just about the legendary leaders — Disney, Wells, Eisner, et al. The tales include the exploits of chambermaids, street cleaners, monorail drivers, and hourly costumed workers. The stories usually chronicle the distinguished deeds of ordinary people.

Some non-Disney corporate managers seem to feel that this technique is great for a fun place like Disney

World but not so effective for, say, a hospital or electric company. Valerie Oberle, vice president of Disney University (DU), believes storytelling has universal application and value.

Once during intermission from a planning session with this writer, Ms. Oberle stopped in to visit one of Disney University's executive seminars. These popular seminars are offered regularly and attended by managers from corporations all over the world. When she can, Valerie makes it a practice to drop in for a few minutes at sessions to answer questions from Disney University's guests and to keep her fingers on the pulse of the corporate world.

> *Gossip and the grapevine function at full volume regardless of whether the management of a company likes it or not. It is obviously to a company's advantage to use that medium to convey desired corporate and cultural messages.*

In this instance, a human resources administrator from a Minnesota utilities company said he was having a problem with the idea of storytelling. Although he was immensely interested in the numerous ways Disney World motivates and involves its cast members, he nevertheless confessed: "If I go back and tell my boss that the secret to a customer service corporate culture is storytelling, he'd be convinced I've been down here on a boondoggle. Other than storytelling, what should we do?" Ms. Oberle studied the question for a long moment and responded: "Well, if you don't tell stories, what are you going to do?" He searched for an answer and had none. She continued, answering her own rhetorical question: "If you don't tell stories — you're going to tell stories."

The point is clear that gossip and the grapevine function at full volume regardless of whether the management of a company likes it or not. It is obviously to a company's advantage to use the grapevine as a communications medium for its own conduit of positive, constructive and informative stories which convey desired corporate and cultural messages.

As stories permeate the grapevine and begin affecting the culture, myths begin to evolve. A myth is not restricted to tribes, religions, or societies. Myths live within the society of business. As Durkheim noted, our corporations have in many ways become society for their workers. Employee beliefs and value structures are significantly impacted by the surroundings of the workplace — replete with its rumors, legends, ceremonies, and myths.

Employee beliefs and value structures are significantly impacted by the surroundings of the workplace — replete with its rumors, legends, ceremonies, and myths.

Walt Disney World is just such a society. It covers forty square miles near Orlando and with 35,000 employees is a legal municipality in Florida. It has its own electric company and water works, its own mayor (appointed by the corporation and recognized by the State of Florida) and it is totally dependent on tourism. It has more than 22,000 hotel rooms and — importantly — it has stories that circulate throughout its entire infrastructure with seamless synergy.

Port Orleans is one of the many themed hotel complexes at Disney World. There is a story about a chambermaid who, in straightening up a room, found stuffed animals that the children had gathered and scattered about the floor. The family was not in the room when the woman began cleaning. As she finished, she tucked the stuffed animals between bedspread and pillows, and left a note saying, "They were having a good time but were too tired to wait up for you," and signed her name.

When the family returned the kids were elated. The parents were so impressed they thanked the hotel staff and later, upon returning home, sent a letter relating how much the trip meant to them. As a closing note they mentioned that one of their children was extremely ill and not likely to live much longer. Disney World was the memory of her life and notably her family's. As the word moved through the Disney circuitry, chambermaids began arranging dolls and stuffed animals on chairs, around TV sets, in beds, building a tradition from one thoughtful worker's inspired sense of moment and gesture. And from there, as before, storytelling continued.

Stories can, and should be, managed. Tactics without strategies become activities without a support foundation. Internal marketing must direct the strategy. No one can go to Disney World, scoop up on a few motivational tactics (like storytelling, for one) and return home with enough Pixie Dust to solve a company's cultural problems. Such change requires research and planning. It also requires commitment from the top, not just the middle.

Stories and oral traditions are part of a corporation's momentum — the human drive that moves leadership at the top and spreads quality performance messages through all layers of the organization.

Consistently executing the concepts of a cultural plan helps make stories, legends and, ultimately, heroes fixtures in the psyche of an organization. Building character is not a six-month program or a theme for a back-to-basics convention speech. It's a *raison d'etre* — and it must be planned and pursued.

I remember an observation made by Kit Wohl, an advertising agency executive who worked with me during my decade-plus at Popeyes Fried Chicken. During one exhaustive, late night meeting, she said in frustration and near seriousness, "policy around here is made by rumor." Don't discount the power of the spoken word. It has sunk many politicians and has helped to build many kingdoms — even Magic Kingdoms.

CHAPTER

8

PARADIGM ANALYSIS:
IN SEARCH OF THE CULTURAL GRAIL

PARADIGM
ANALYSIS
In Search of the Cultural Grail

"Do thou hasten to King Arthur, and charge him from me to undertake, without delay, the quest of the Sacred Grail. The knight is already born, and has received knighthood at his hands, who is destined to accomplish this quest."

— *Merlin to Sir Gawain*

The thirteenth-century Vulgate Cycle first made mention of Galahad, the knight known for achieving the quest for the Holy Grail. Galahad and the Grail have both become associated with noble crusades and worthwhile endeavors. Achieving a base of values in a company is a quest as well, an arduous and worthy task which should inspire those involved.

DEFINING THE PARADIGM
If we imagine enterprise as a quest, it must begin with an understanding of where the seeker (management) is located and what terrain must be traveled to reach the goal. The search should start with an analysis of the corporate paradigm. The word *paradigm* has been discussed at considerable length in recent years as it has

moved into business vocabulary. There are numerous
definitions of the word — not only of the standard
dictionary variety, but also specialized meanings. Some
say it has become a buzzword, devalued through overuse
and misuse. Agreed, it has been abused, but I maintain
that it is nonetheless a useful and important word. For
the purpose of this writing, I propose my own definition
and beg the reader's indulgence for the sake of discussion.

> **paradigm:** all the factors that combine to
> make a company what it is.

This definition takes an existential view of the term.
Every company has a paradigm by the very fact that the
company exists. The paradigm may not be well defined
or well known — and it may not be what is desired — but
it exists nonetheless. This fact is irrefutable. Moreover,
the paradigm is controllable and manageable. Author
Thomas Kuhn posits that a paradigm should be a
scientific, predictable model; the actions and reactions
of an organization should be the logical result of a clearly
structured paradigm. A company's paradigm can be
molded, for better or worse. If the paradigm of a company
is ignored and the organizational parts are not in
harmony, the operation turns messy.

THE PARADIGM FACTORS
International Marketing Systems subdivides the *factors*
of the paradigm into three categories: functional,
environmental, and cultural. Functional matters define
how a company gets its work done, the nuts and bolts of
operations (product preparation/production,
organizational charts, training procedures, etc.). The
environmental factors include all the outside influences
in a company's life and its interaction with these influences
(advertising, consumer trends, competitive activity, etc.).
The cultural aspects of a company describe how its

members think, act, and feel as a group and as individual members of the group (values, emotions, philosophies, and beliefs).

Many smart companies methodically address the functional and environmental issues of importance but do not systematically deal with the cultural matters, which I contend comprise the most important factor of the paradigm. It is somewhat like building a car without a steering wheel. The corporate culture provides the direction to guide the mechanical functions of the organization. Moreover, as one client put it, "it is more likely we can work our company out of a functional problem with a strong culture than it is likely we can evolve our company out of a competitive crisis with a weak culture and undedicated workforce."

Don Smith, past president of both McDonald's and Burger King once said: "I'd rather have a well executed mediocre business plan than a poorly executed great business plan." It takes dedicated people to execute any type of plan well. And dedication doesn't last long if the culture goes untended.

> *"I'd rather have a well executed mediocre business plan than a poorly executed great business plan."*
> *— **Don Smith**, past president of both McDonald's and Burger King.*

DOCUMENTING THE PARADIGM

A paradigm analysis, then, is an audit of the three categories and an analysis of the key issues involved. Data for such an analysis is acquired through primary and secondary research. Of particular note and emphasis should be the cultural analysis, for it has most likely been the most overlooked segment in previous plans and activities. It should include vertical and horizontal canvassing of the organization, from CEO to hourly workers and across all departmental lines. The object is

> *Done correctly, the paradigm analysis is more than a fact-gathering effort. It becomes the first step in getting the various layers of employees to join the process of launching a cultural initiative.*

to get a well rounded view of the philosophical universe that is as objective and candid as possible.

It's not at all uncommon to find upper management feeling that the mission and motivations of a company are understood clearly in the lower ranks — only to have them discover (to their surprise) that the cultural audit indicates rank and file perceptions are 180° in a different direction.

Often it is more effective to have someone outside of the company conduct the analysis to ensure objectivity. Perceived objectivity of the plan is important to all stakeholders as they consider whether to embrace an internal marketing initiative. Using an outsider to facilitate fact-finding focus group sessions also gives employees somewhat of an insulated comfort zone, should they have some controversial observations to volunteer. Besides, not many companies have a bunch of folks waiting around to conduct a paradigm analysis.

Done correctly, the paradigm analysis is more than a fact-gathering effort. It becomes the first step in getting the various layers of employees to join the process of launching a cultural initiative. When they have an opportunity to participate by giving their views in focus groups and interviews, a sense of emotional equity in the initiative spreads among the staff.

Compiled into a structured document, the paradigm analysis becomes a guide for cultural strategic planning.

TEXACO IN THE THIRD WORLD

A Classic Paradigm Case Study

When a company operates internationally, the development of a paradigm analysis can pose difficult challenges. American business standards, however widely emulated, must be weighed against local traditions. Standard methods of accounting are reasonably uniform; motivating a foreign employee base to market American products with can-do zeal is another matter — and it can prove an imposing task.

Consider the case of Texaco's retailing efforts in Latin America and West Africa (LA/WA). When International Marketing Systems was hired by then International Vice President of Marketing Steve O'Farrell to help strengthen the LA/WA service and field marketing efforts, the preliminary hurdle proved to be cultural: how to convey the message of an American multinational's service and marketing ethic in regions of the world where the behavior was largely foreign? The ultimate challenge was to imbue Third World service station operations with an idea of salesmanship extending beyond the simple across-the-counter transactions for gasoline and engine oil. Moreover, early research showed that the environment of many stations lagged behind American outlets in efficiency and cleanliness.

In the research phase, through hundreds of interviews in the field (in literally dozens of developing countries) and with regional managers, IMS staff found a retail culture that had no real grasp of the parent corporation's history, much less an appreciation of shared goals and responsibilities — no linkage of a retail outlet's employees to the brand.

In many African and Central American outlets, Texaco had people thrilled to have a low-level entry job; yet they also had no comprehension of service or *suggestive selling* or *total customer*

(Continued on next page)

(Continued from previous page)

satisfaction. The long-term challenge was to shift the supply-driven paradigm of field retailing to one that was more marketing and service-driven.

For Texaco LA/WA, International Marketing Systems helped construct and conduct a detailed series of seminars on how successful operations rely on core marketing principles in training their employees. This message needed context, though. We found a disconnect in the field infrastructure linking headquarters and the retail level. At the field level of retail operations, the workers' ties were to the owners of gas stations, the bosses who wrote the paychecks.

We designed a system of Field Marketing Coordinators (FMCs), trained by headquarters in the areas of business consultation. FMCs were then given field marketing packages and market data for conducting meetings with their sales reps. The sales reps' dealers were then motivated to pass information and programs down to the pump attendants and cashiers, people on the ground floor, giving them a sense of their own stake in the enterprise.

Industry research shows that when a motorist sees a Shell, Mobil or a Texaco station (or any other competitive gasoline station) on the same road, the driver considers the gasoline quality to be the same. What explains the decision to choose one brand over the other? Assuming the convenience factor is identical, much of the answer lies in ***service***: *a sense of personal connection between the local people who sell the product and the customer* (motorist). **That is retailing!** By communicating such information to the operators, who in turn are supplied a system to share sales and service-building tactics with their workers, a service-ethic culture began to take root. LA/WA's John Thwing was charged with coordinating the distribution of this concept and materials to the field. For over seven years now the Star Field Marketing System (SFMS) has been reinforcing these service and retail philosophies, a process that, over time, has positively impacted profitability. It took seven years of commitment. It was not a program du jour. And at Texaco LA/WA, the trends continue in a most impressive way.

INTERNAL MARKETING
STRATEGIC PLANNING

INTERNAL MARKETING
STRATEGIC PLANNING
Time Traveling

"Ah, yes. How did I know to set breakfast for two? Now ordinary people are born forwards in Time, if you understand what I mean, and nearly everything in the world goes forward, too. This makes it quite easy for ordinary people to live. But unfortunately, I was born at the wrong end of time, and I have to live backwards from in front, while surrounded by a lot of people living forward from behind."
— Merlin to King Arthur

T. H. White's *Once and Future King* portrays Merlin the Wizard, mentor to the young King Arthur, as a man with prescience, an uncanny sense of knowing what will happen before it occurs. Charles E. Smith, Ph.D. coined a term — The Merlin Factor — in a description of "future-first" perspective. Dr. Smith writes: "The Merlin Factor is the process whereby leaders transform themselves and the culture of their organizations through a creative commitment to a radically different future." It also refers to a technique of planning which looks at the future first, determining the result desired, then systematically laying

> *The ability to move ahead in time and see the future as it will (or can) be is the essence of strategic planning for internal marketing. The crux lies in shaping that vision and charting the course to achieve it.*

out the necessary steps to reach the objective. The ability to move ahead in time and see the future as it will (or can) be is the essence of strategic planning for internal marketing. The crux lies in shaping that vision and charting the course to achieve it.

STRATEGIC PLAN FOR INTERNAL MARKETING

With the paradigm analysis providing essential insights, cultural strategic planning targets the issues of the future. The cultural strategic plan, or internal marketing plan, defines the vision ("where we're going") and the mission ("how we'll get there"). It translates the abstract concepts of the vision and mission into an action-oriented plan.

The goals, objectives, strategies, and tactics are detailed for each aspect of the paradigm. With the tenets and tasks spelled out in an orderly fashion, the goals begin to take on the shape of reality.

A cultural strategic plan is distinguished from financially-directed plans (business plan, marketing plan, expansion plan, etc.) in that internal marketing deals with issues of philosophy, people, and the inner dynamics that make workers productive and proud of what they do. Both types of planning are critical and not mutually exclusive. They must complement each other. The cultural plan is not "feel good" or "warm and fuzzy"; rather, it's a process to boost employee morale and productivity. It is a call to action, infused with tactics designed to translate theory into practice which will bolster bottom line performance. It will be sales-focused and conceived as a trackable vehicle for building business and performance.

BUT WILL THEY BUY INTO IT ACROSS THE RANKS?

To achieve the greatest impact, a strategic plan for internal marketing (cultural development) should include input and participation by a vertical cut of the organization. In tactical development particularly, the operational people (middle managers, supervisors, etc.) who actually do the work and more often interact with guests or customers on the firing line, can be a better source of information and insight about what will work (and what won't) than can high-level executives. Input and views from upper management are, of course, important, though usually on a more strategic level.

BLUEPRINT FOR BUILDING A CULTURE

When it is complete and approved by management, the internal marketing plan serves as a blueprint for building the values-based corporate culture. It shows how to go about the construction or support of the desired corporate culture, what raw materials are needed, and how they should be assembled. It provides for concrete, measurable improvements in customer service and satisfaction levels, repeat customer count, and lower employee turnover (with reduced training and replacement expense). The strategic plan enables the company to move confidently towards exceeding customer expectations and the resulting improvement in sales and profits, thereby meeting shareholder expectations.

CHAPTER

10

MOBILIZATION:
CAMELOT'S CHAMPIONS

MOBILIZATION
Camelot's Champions

*"I shall summon unto Camelot the most keen
and worthy knights of the realm. And they
will suppe wythe me at a grate table which
shall be rounde, then each shall be nue more
honoured than another seated there, but they
shall know honours by the solemn quests they
champion and fulfille."*
— **King Arthur to Merlin**

Mobilization of internal marketing activity is the make-
or-break step in the culture-building process. Even the
most inspired and brilliant strategic plan only amounts
to mental aerobics until it is actually put into action. On
the other hand, even a mediocre strategic plan,
enthusiastically carried out, can move the needle and
make a difference.

ENERGY FLOWS FROM THE TOP
Mobilization starts with a total commitment from top
management. The CEO must be convinced that the
process is useful and wholeheartedly embrace the tenets
of the strategic plan. After all of the input and discussion,
the CEO probably makes the final call on what the
company stands for, and what its vision should be. For
the plan to succeed, the CEO's conviction must be evident

to all of management — upper, middle and lower.

EMPLOYEE INVOLVEMENT

In a healthy company, *champions* will emerge from the middle and lower ranks — managers and supervisors drawn to the visionary objectives of upper management because they recognize a path to greater earnings for themselves and they believe that it is right. These men and women will increase productivity and sales if their hearts are in it and they feel unified. Top management should inspire their confidence by making the corporation's mission statement a reality, a touchstone of the culture.

You can't successfully order people to smile and mandate them to exceed customer expectations. Likewise, you can't order troops to follow; you have to lead them!

Care must be taken so that everyone — even hourly employees — embraces the initiative, rather than thrusting it upon people from above, in a way that feels forced and artificial. The sense of genuine bonding to a concept will be far more effective in the workers' execution of the plan if they believe in it as something that is in their interest, rather than just another order to be followed. You can't successfully order people to smile and mandate them to exceed customer expectations; just as you can't order troops to follow, you have to lead them!

In large corporations, the nurturing of champions should cultivate an *esprit de corps*. In the pharmaceutical industry, as Tom Peters and Nancy Austin have written, "scientific discovery is highly-visible; the clinical wizards receive their share of praise and rewards. But the 'last 90 percent' of the production and marketing process, so crucial to profits, has its share of unsung heroes." These are the champions. These people, Peters and Austin explain "can cut more time from the total process than the genius of the discovery phase. For instance, he or she can drum up support for the drug among members of the medical establishment, push and cajole the clinical testers [and] often reduce the normal clearance time by as much as 75 percent, if they energetically pursue their tasks."

Energy is key to the champion-building process that an internal marketing plan puts forth. It should be a positive current of energy, not driven by back-stabbing, internecine squabbles, or political jockeying that envelop many corporations. The initiative to build and sustain a values-based culture needs champions who are productive and visionary, yes; but they should have a moral sensibility too, a sense of right and wrong about life and about what's best for the company where they work. Like medieval knights they will see an initiative through, fend off the obstacles, and influence their fellow workers by example.

Put another way, champions should be activists for the internal culture of the company. If each company is its own Camelot, the lessons of King Arthur and his Round Table counsel the nurturing of these high-achievers and natural leaders within the corporate walls. Moreover, the contemporary model of society should include women in all aspects of the company's performance, and reward them accordingly.

CULTIVATING CHAMPIONS

Leaders on all levels will surface at different times and under different circumstances. They should be encouraged and given recognition as they grow into their role as champions, creating motion and driving the company to greater performance and profits. The strategic plan should have systems for using those champions as disciples of the culture and tactics for recognizing their efforts.

COMMUNICATING THE CULTURE

The principal tool of mobilization is communication, especially cultural communication. Communication only occurs when a bit of information or an idea has been successfully transferred from one person's mind to another's. Circulating memos can often be merely shuffling information. For cultural development and incubating values, communication techniques that ensure a connection are required.

A successful internal marketing plan will have numerous communication strategies and tactics — each with its own strength and technique for touching the minds and hearts of the company members by reinforcing its values. As discussed earlier, one such tactic is storytelling. Storytelling uses anecdotes, metaphors, myths, and legends to make points real and personal. Many great teachers have used the power of stories to communicate values — Aesop with his fables, Abe Lincoln with his folksy yarns, Jesus of Nazareth with his parables. In a well-balanced internal marketing system, storytelling is a thread of philosophical continuity between the organization's past and present. But an organization needs to be able to rely methodically on the right type of people to step forward at key times and tell those stories.

Champions should be activists for the internal culture of the company.

AMBASSADORS

A well-designed cultural initiative uses peer communication for dissemination of stories and more plotted information. At IMS we refer to the insightful individuals who are carefully trained as peer communicators as "Ambassadors." Peer communication has the advantage of perceived credibility: the sharing of a common language from a common point of view, one hourly or line-level worker to another. It can be purely informal or meticulously planned. It can rely mainly on the grapevine, which is active in every company that has more than two people working, or it can be developed (planned) with specially trained "Ambassadors" who act as seed carriers for value-based information within an organization.

VERTICAL INTEGRATION

Beyond storytelling and peer communicators (ambassadors), an essential feature of a communications effort is vertical integration. Communication tactics should be coordinated on multiple levels to achieve maximum impact and synergy. It's similar to principles used in consumer marketing. A professionally designed external (consumer) marketing plan plots and thematically coordinates television and radio spots, newspaper ads, outdoor boards, in-store promotions, and other media. The idea is to be sure people see variations of the same advertising message on a number of occasions from a number of sources. The same technique applies to internal marketing.

Communication only occurs when a bit of information or an idea has been successfully transferred from one person's mind to another's.

REACH AND FREQUENCY IN INTERNAL MARKETING

In planning events to influence a corporate culture, internal marketing borrows two important concepts from external marketing: reach and frequency. These are traditional media-buying terms to describe the degree of penetration and impact a message potentially has on its intended target audience (in our case, a company's internal audience — the employees). *Reach* refers to the portion of the target audience that is exposed to a message, usually noted as a percentage. In advertising, a 70% reach would mean that seven out of ten members of the target audience would receive some exposure to the message. *Frequency* quantifies how many times an average individual in the target audience is exposed to the message. Together, reach and frequency drive the effectiveness of a campaign (although, the content and creative positioning of the advertising carry ultimate importance). Internal media (the myriad of vehicles for communications) can be built into a vertically integrated marketing system in much the same way that advertising is directed at non-employees.

Reportedly, J. C. Penney once said: "I know that 50% of our advertising is effective; the problem is I don't know which 50%." Repetition from various fronts (redundancy) and continuous exposure to the message are as essential internally as they are externally.

Redundancy and continuous exposure to the message are as essential internally as they are externally.

THE PARTNERSHIP OF THE SERVICE AND MARKETING MISSIONS

The service mission of a company — how its employees answer the needs of its customers — should complement its marketing mission and help build business. And then, with repetition, it must be *sold into* the internal target audience (employees).

Companies that are good, consistent marketers work hard at building and maintaining their image; it evolves into a *feel* — a *style*. The best internal marketing strategy builds on the strengths of that style. The image should integrate into the internal marketing of the company's identity. A good example of such a strategy at its best is the marketing culture at McDonald's.

Everyone knows that McDonald's sells hamburgers. But the company's phenomenal success stems from a customer service approach to sales, rather than the mindset of a product-driven fast food chain. This marketing-driven identity resonates inside the organization, working its way into the outer image of the company through advertising and promotions.

McDonald's TV spots always show smiling faces and

prompt service. McDonald's knows that smiling faces don't just happen by the luck of the draw. The entire retail system revolves around the premise of exceeding the service expectations of customers. That's why one can't buy a McDonald's franchise unless one is willing to run one of the restaurants as a hands-on owner. The company's culture is not that of the absentee investor. It is one of personal commitment — even from its millionaire franchise owners. The corporate identity is inextricably linked to the advertising you see — a well honed, customer service, retail, marketing machine.

At Hamburger U. in Oakbrook, Illinois, the marketing mission of McDonald's is clearly defined: superior customer service. That's the anchor of the organization.

When the franchisees mandatorily attend and graduate from Hamburger U. (before taking control of their operation), they aren't just taught how to operate a hamburger stand. They've learned those skills in the McDonald's system for weeks and months before, out in the field and on the job. No, Hamburger U. imbues both franchisees and operators with the philosophy, culture, and service credo of the company. It comes from all directions, with an appreciation for reach and frequency. *The internal message never stops!*

McDonald's phenomenal success stems from a customer service approach to sales, rather than the mindset of a product-driven fast food chain.

The service, marketing vision, and discipline of the operation show through on the firing line — the customer contact point. Let's look at one example of how the external marketing mission and the internal marketing culture ultimately join.

Fast food outlets feature promotional games (such as rub-off collector coupons) as part of their marketing strategy. Typically, a company advertises to make the rub-off game appear exciting and to create awareness that something new is going on. The real target of such a marketing tactic is to increase volume — to make people like the game enough to come back more often during the game's time cycle. Theoretically, the marketing tool should increase the number of visits by the same customer and the size of the average check on a given purchase regardless of whether the advertising supporting the game motivates new users to come into the restaurant.

McDonald's has legions of internal marketers — cooks, cashiers, service workers — who turn the game into an event. They know they're not supposed to wait for people to ask for the coupons. McDonald's' employees know their job is to complement the marketing mission. And, unlike scores of other chains (where the corporate cultures are more product driven), when McDonald's promotes a rub-off game, they can expect the system to experience a significant short-term spike in sales regardless of how good or mediocre the ad campaign happens to be. Their people make it happen; they get the game pieces

> *McDonald's has legions of internal marketers — employees who know their job is to complement the marketing mission.*

distributed to their existing customer base, as well as to those coming in specifically for the game.

I remember years ago at Popeyes, after we had just conducted one of those rub-off promotions, a manager of one of the company-owned stores called the advertising department. The question was, "What do I do with the box of left over game cards in the back office; not enough customers came in and asked for them?!" The point is so easily lost, unless one commits to a systematic methodology of internal marketing and follow-up communications. The culture makes it or breaks it!

Put another way, operations and advertising should work symbiotically, wedded to the same concept. It's not a test to see if advertising is bringing in new customers. The operations group must mesh with the marketing. McDonald's may be a hamburger company, but they are committed to a service- and marketing-oriented corporate culture. They are not supply-driven as a culture; they are marketing and retail driven.

CASE STUDY

11

A PATHWAY TO SUCCESS

A PATHWAY TO SUCCESS
Empress Casino

Casino gambling is a growth industry of the '90s. Its news media image — or reputation, if you will — is mixed. As one set of elected officials has turned to gaming taxes for sorely needed revenues, still other political figures condemn gambling as a quick-fix approach to the budget crises that seem unending. From a practical business standpoint, three observations can be made.

Since the '80s, there have been major shifts in the gaming industry. Along with business legitimacy has come a significant shift to a service focus.

First, the old image of mafia gangsters running casinos is fading, as a new generation of managers, many with business school skills, have taken management roles in casinos in Las Vegas, Atlantic City, and elsewhere. Overall, the industry is run in the more businesslike fashion that Wall Street expects of publicly traded companies. Since the '80s, there have been major shifts in the gaming industry. Along with market acceptance has come a significant shift to a service focus. Led by such luminaries as Steve Wynn of the prestigious Mirage organization, the industry has evolved into an entertainment offering. In the emerging gaming markets of the Midwest, South, and New England, the glare of the public spotlight on gaming operations leaves few hiding places and holds gaming operations to a much higher standard of discipline and business management integrity than most unregulated businesses in the community.

Second, the marketing of many casinos today has focused on gaming as an entertainment attraction for broader-based family tourism, selling the gambling side as part of a larger package of resort environments with games and activities for adults and, more and more often, ancillary considerations for children. The resplendent, fantastically themed resort megaliths cropping up in Las Vegas are an indication of how far the industry has evolved from the smoke-filled gambling hall image. Mirage's Wynn makes it clear that he admires the Disney organization and subscribes to the Disney ideology of customer satisfaction, even incorporating much of its doctrine into his own organization.

Many casinos market gaming as an entertainment attraction for broader-based family tourism, selling the gambling side as part of a larger package of resort environments with games and activities for adults and ancillary considerations for children.

Third, in emerging gaming markets, political chicanery is often a natural accompaniment for the gambling temptation when it comes to town. Everybody expects prolific financial activity and too many have a hand out, wanting a piece of the action. The casinos are often viewed as the cash cow to solve all the local infrastructure ills. Sometimes with so many honorariums, chances of the operation's success are diminished — witness the bankruptcy of Harrah's Jazz in New Orleans, which as of early 1996, was an inactive volcano of controversy. Excessive contributions to the city and state coffers as required of the casino's parent company, along with a tax rate that would be considered intolerable for any other type of business, combined with lower than projected revenues, spelled failure.

Nevertheless, gambling-as-tourism is an economic force in many states that is unlikely to dissipate. The expanding horizon of gaming seems to work best in outer-city, small- and medium-sized communities, like the Mississippi Gulf Coast, where the local economies need the jobs and indirect benefits spin off from a big tourist outlet.

As a case in point, unlike the "banana republic" modus operandi found in some gaming jurisdictions, Mississippi has proven to be more progressive in its approach to the gaming market. By allowing free and unlimited competition on an open market, Mississippi exercises a more limited regulatory control of the industry, leaving it to sort itself out according to the age-old laws of supply and demand. There have been some casino failures in the shake-out, but what remains is a stable industry. The consequence for the state and the communities where there are casinos is the presence of a cash cow with little, if any, scandal.

Gambling-as-tourism is an economic force in many states that is unlikely to dissipate.

With this proliferation of gaming destinations surfacing within the industry, high employee turnover driven by an expanding market is an ongoing headache. It is expensive to train carddealers, roulettewheel operators, and others to work the gaming floor and food service areas if people keep moving on to newer, fresher facilities for better perceived working conditions and benefits, better *tokes* (tips) which often come at a newly opened facility, and sometimes just a grass-is-greener attitude. As noted earlier, when Empress River Casino opened in Joliet, Illinois, Kevin Larson believed that, to ensure long-term success in an increasingly competitive marketplace, satisfied casino visitors must be motivated to return. He felt that the key to providing guest satisfaction of such magnitude is to foster a working environment that keeps employees

satisfied. With satisfied employees who believe in the organization and in themselves, the environment creates a desire to make guests happy. Without a strong sense of self-worth by the employees, great service will not happen no matter how many memos get sent out or pep meetings get held. As International Marketing Systems worked with Empress's executive management to develop an internal marketing plan, we found a rare opportunity. Although Empress was a 2,000-employee operation, modeled on Las Vegas casinos (with an elaborate Egyptian motif), the company had only a brief history and a very limited legacy, given its two years in business. The challenge was to design a cultural blueprint, create an environment that resonated an employee-valued sensibility, in other words, to craft a legacy. Kevin referred to this as a *footprint*. IMS looked at this as a creative opportunity.

An internal monitoring system for motivation measures the effectiveness of the Pathway system at regular intervals, with follow-up surveys to gauge progress of the internal marketing initiative.

Our plan for Empress involved internal dynamics that hinged on a small group of communications specialists, hired specifically to serve as conduits of information (ambassadors to and for their peers) and to help inculcate the Empress Footprint in the company. These enthusiastic employees were referred to, by their spirited and supportive peers as Foot Doctors. Their job was to enhance communication between top-level management and line-level employees. The overall communications process was referred to as the *Pathway*. An internal monitoring system for motivation measures the effectiveness of the Pathway system at regular intervals, with follow-up surveys to gauge progress of the internal marketing initiative.

In an orientation video, IMS introduced the metaphor of the Pathway and stories about epic achievements of a mythical kingdom designed to drive home deeper messages about the business and Kevin's perception of what Empress' corporate values should be. These values included:

- **Caring** about others (fellow employees and customers on the gaming floor) and about one's job and doing it well;
- **Respect** for oneself, co-workers, and guests;
- **Integrity** in dealing with others, personal honesty, openness, and fairness.

During the Empress orientation process the footprint is used as an emblem to promote the building of a career-long commitment to the organization. The corporate motto reads: "These values, The Empress Footprint, are the markers that will guide us as we make our way forward." Last I checked, footprints were being emblazoned throughout the operation, in the employees' line of vision, as subtle reminders of a culture that cares.

Ultimately, the long-term benefits of the Empress efforts will depend upon the continued commitment that ownership and management pay to the system. Reinforcement and repetition of the core values of the Empress Footprint and sustained efforts to nurture the Pathway of internal communication will ensure a progressively evolving corporate and service culture.

A PRESCRIPTION

RECONNECTING THE HEART AND SOUL
OF AMERICAN BUSINESS

RECONNECTING THE HEART AND SOUL OF AMERICAN BUSINESS

A Prescription

Companies like McDonald's, Walt Disney World, FedEx, Ritz-Carlton, and others are proving that strong values-based cultures are profitably successful and these companies become the ones other organizations admire and try to emulate. But simply studying how they do it at Disney or FedEx or the Ritz is not enough. Knowing the techniques is not the same as understanding and believing in the values. It's like the difference between knowledge and wisdom. To be wise one must own knowledge, practice it and imbibe. Wisdom is experiential. Values and commitment are the heart and soul of these successful companies. It is having champions who understand the big picture that keeps their cultures active and vibrant. It is learning to build clocks rather than telling time. Techniques and tactics can change. The vision remains constant.

> *To be wise one must own knowledge, practice it and imbibe. Wisdom is experiential.*

A CLEARER VISION

To be more competitive at home and on the world market, the individual leaders of American business must broaden their vision beyond the quarterly dividend spreadsheet and look at what the business universe demands.

Management must reward and welcome the champions who rise through the ranks to become heroes, those who perform deeds that create legends. They must have the courage to act out of conviction, not for ovations. They must be authentic people. Historian Daniel Boorstin notes: "The hero is known for achievements, the celebrity for well-knownness. The hero reveals the possibilities of human nature, the celebrity reveals the possibilities of the press and the media. Celebrities are people who make the news, but heroes are people who make history. Time makes heroes but dissolves celebrities."

"The hero is known for achievements, the celebrity for well-knownness. The hero reveals the possibilities of human nature, the celebrity reveals the possibilities of the press and the media. Celebrities are people who make the news, but heroes are people who make history. Time makes heroes but dissolves celebrities."

— Daniel Boorstin

PEOPLE STILL COUNT IN A TECHNOLOGICAL WORLD

Wise leaders recognize that — no matter how sophisticated their technologies or how successful their last quarter's performance — theirs is still a company of people. The wise leaders look inward and strive to maintain an enduring connection with their members. At Starbucks, the wildly successful coffeehouse chain, the customer doesn't come first, the employee does. Starbucks CEO Howard Schultz says: "I think what American companies have failed to realize is that there's tremendous value in getting everyone in the company to share a common purpose of self-esteem, self-respect, and appreciation. It's just good business as well as the right thing to do."

Today's corporation is an entity that is both social and financial. What keeps the two sides close and working together is a sense of common goals, shared by the various human levels. If the corporation is to make the best of its role as a surrogate tribe of modern social orders, the connective tissue among all its members must be recognized, nurtured, and internalized by the executives who make decisions and guide the strategy.

Involvement and understanding the business and human quest must be communicated and sold in to the ranks of middle management — many of whom have grown accustomed to thinking of employees as a cost of doing business, rather than as allies in a common goal. *The chieftains of the* This is not to imply some socialistic view that the corporate world exists in order to *new tribes should* supply employment for the masses. No, *search within to* corporate America does not owe anyone a job. Capitalism calls for hard work and *understand the true* having every individual carry his or her *and lasting values for* own weight. Individual initiative is part *which their* of the inherent responsibility that belongs in every corporate body. However, a *companies should* shared cause is the single most galvanizing *stand, the heart and* element in the lives of the employees and stakeholders of a company. That is true *soul of their* empowerment. *organizations.*

It is incumbent on the corporation to satisfy the needs for norms of conduct, civility, and morality that so many of our religious leaders, elected officials, and columnists find in short supply. The biggest, most successful corporations are not in the business of saving the world, but they do build values-based corporate cultures. Their business is providing goods and services that enhance their customers' lives.

Make no mistake of it, the motivation to act is pragmatic as well as humanitarian. For business to prosper, it must have healthy markets and willing buyers. When people (consumers) are positive and upbeat, they spend. When they aren't, they don't. The principles of internal marketing are a step toward ensuring a rewarding frame of mind for the employees of a company, thus creating a positive atmosphere for the consumer. The result: increased business from customers who are satisfied by superior service and a "come again" experience. It doesn't happen by accident. It happens because the visionaries of a company take the right actions to make it happen over the long haul.

The chieftains of the new tribes should search within to understand the true and lasting values for which their companies should stand, the heart and soul of their organizations.

That makes for good business and an ever-responsive customer base.

EPILOGUE

MAKE YOUR OWN MAGIC

MAKE YOUR OWN MAGIC
Epilogue

From its inception, I worked at creating and sustaining an image for Popeyes Famous Fried Chicken — a fast food chain founded in New Orleans by Al Copeland. In the early days, we steadfastly nurtured the company's creative position of being anchored in the culinary and diverse ethnic heritage of that unique town. The city's pungent recipes and cultural novelties were the emotional epicenter of the spicy chicken chain's early competitive differentiation.

To that point, I recall one evening I was screening a newly-produced commercial to Copeland and some of our management team. The filming had recreated a lively French Quarter Jazz Funeral band marching out of a Popeyes restaurant. The band had a crowd of customers dancing down the street behind it. In the black New Orleans culture, this ritual, the *second line*, refers to a celebration of life — the spirit is joyously ascending to its proper place. This television spot was as spirited as the chicken. One of the department heads in the room commented that he didn't think jazz bands had much to do with selling two pieces of spicy chicken with Cajun "dirty rice" and a roll for 89 cents. So, we talked imagery for a while.

Later, I reflected that lots of folks don't think about or possibly understand imagery (let alone identity). More

Popeyes was capturing magic and putting it successfully into a bottle. Externally and internally, Popeyes was on an experiential roll.

importantly, I began to develop further the view that this unique Popeyes image positioning of vitality, spirit and flavor wasn't confined only to the advertising campaign and our product line. Behind the scenes, there was cult-like bonding by franchisees and employees alike to the zealous identity behind the image. Customers followed suit; they felt it, too. Popeyes was capturing magic and putting it successfully into one of Howard Gossage's bottles. Externally and internally, Popeyes was on an experiential roll.

This was like the early days of Coors beer when customers would cross over state lines to fill ice chests full of that magic brew and bring it home to the excitement of partying friends. Well, the Popeyes spot ran and it — along with the longer term campaign — was a smashing success.

In the early 1970s, when I started this conceptual positioning and brand management quest, there were less than a dozen Popeyes stores. When I moved on, Popeyes had 1,000 stores in its sights and Al was keenly focused on the billion dollar mark in sales. That didn't successfully happen, though.

Some six months after I left Popeyes, Copeland bought rival chicken chain Church's. Two years later, amid franchisee consternation from both brand camps (Popeyes and Church's), bankruptcy protection and lawsuits from investment bankers, Al Copeland lost his company.

Although by then I was long gone, I did watch on with interest.

Right from the takeover, the banks, still smarting from the contentious negotiations with Copeland, and their management team began to purge the company of the legacy and heritage that was so integral to the psyche of Popeyes. To public view, it appeared they wanted the company to have no part of Al Copeland or his past — including New Orleans. A crowning blow to this assault on identity came when they uprooted this New Orleans style chicken chain's headquarters and moved its hundreds of jobs over to southern rival Atlanta — sufficiently distanced from Al Copeland, but unfortunately, far removed from the brand's roots. (Somehow I doubt if someday we'd find Kentucky Fried Chicken's headquarters moved to, say, Nashville, even though some might argue that Nashville is an easier place to get to and has a more expansive business climate than Louisville.)

> *One must realize that it takes visionaries to see beyond financial statements, ego and private agendas, and to appreciate and nurture the metaphysical side of business. An American landscape without visionaries is certainly destined to be a business wasteland.*

It is important for American business to realize that it takes visionaries to see beyond financial statements, ego, and private agendas, and to appreciate and nurture the metaphysical side of business. An American landscape without visionaries is certainly destined to be a business wasteland.

As my own path moved on, I remained very appreciative of all sorts of lessons, knowledge, and skills that those thirteen years at Popeyes taught me. However, the most valuable lessons I learned came from knowing what _wasn't_ done and speculating on what potential was lost.

There was tremendous untapped cultural, marketing and stakeholder potential at Popeyes. But the values and virtue of all those players who at different times controlled Popeyes' destiny gave every evidence of being driven mostly by material, financial, or ego motives. And the heart and soul of this once dynamic company hasn't revived yet. Sadly, Popeyes seems to be heading to being simply another mainstream franchise food service entry. The high ground is dangerously close to being lost. The magic has gone out of the bottle. Yet, the ember of the brand's original spirit still has a faint glow. The current owners show signs of rediscovering some of these elements of cultural magic which are difficult to identify and quantify, realizing that the idea is bigger than the man who created it and separate from the individual. The flames of Popeyes spicy New Orleans heritage may flicker anew. I, for one, would cheer the re-ignition of that spirit.

At some point in life, in reasonable, conservative measures, you too can start moving your ladder closer to that other wall.

Joseph Campbell tells a poignant story of a man who, for a lifetime, climbs the ladder of business and material achievement only to find in his twilight years that the ladder was leaning on the wrong wall.

Campbell was a profound explorer of culture and myth. He was a mentor to George Lucas, director of *Star Wars* (to whom we owe the words "May the force be with you"). In Lucas's film, the "force" proved to be within us all.

At some point in life, in reasonable, conservative measures, you too can start moving your ladder closer to that other wall.

Nearly a decade ago, when leaving Popeyes, I had identified a business niche that motivated me personally and that, I felt and hoped, businesses needed. Several years later when IMS started working with Disney University at Walt Disney World, untold positive reinforcement further energized and helped me crystallize this business vision — to make a difference in the cultures and values of American business.

I close with a story passed on to me by a Disney University Traditions Assistant. This tale may have been filtering through Disney World for some time, as is frequently the way with oral traditions where stories gain momentum through personalization by the tellers. I have taken liberty with the details. But, the meaning prevails.

When I was about five years old, my mother took me to our Main Street Playhouse, the smallest of neighborhood theaters. "Cowboy Bill" was doing a one-man Western show.

Cowboy Bill was a down-on-his-luck vaudevillian, holding on by traveling about entertaining kids and families. Nowadays, he would be akin to finding a 65-year-old clown working birthday parties out of his rundown van.

Well, Cowboy Bill was on stage. The playhouse's twenty-five chairs were filled, standing room only. All during his show I sat in awe. I kept thinking how I could be like Bill, traveling the West, and living a life only dreamt about or seen on TV. I could be up there on stage telling other kids all about it.

But then, Cowboy Bill called for a volunteer from the audience. I was chosen. As I stepped onto that giant stage I became petrified. The arena spotlights were too blinding and all those throngs of people were staring at me. As I stood there, all three feet of me trembling in my Roy Rogers cowboy boots, Bill calmly bent down and gently held my hand. He very kindly gave it a firm squeeze. To my relief I found that the lights weren't as bright any more and the crowd had friendly faces. I could do this! There's nothing to it.

Well, after the show Bill went on to his next stop and probably didn't think back. Wherever he is today, if he's even still alive, he doesn't know of the influence and impact this seemingly insignificant event had on one small kid on Main Street.

Whether you are a C.E.O., corporate visionary, or newly hired clerk in the mail room, never forget the power that one person can have on others. Just by being thoughtful, caring, and active.

I've gone on to give speeches to audiences that have numbered in the thousands and have always remembered that there's nothing to fear. I can do this. Thanks, Bill.

Bill lives on in us all. Whether you are a CEO, corporate visionary, or newly hired clerk in the mail room, never forget the power that one person can have on others. Just by being thoughtful, caring, and active.

Whether you're setting about to build an internal marketing system or getting the mail delivered around the office, remember you can make a difference.

But you have to go beyond thinking about it and you have to actually start doing something about it.

Anomy is not a permanent condition in our contemporary workplace. It's treatable. As seen throughout the pages of this book, life after anomy is personally and professionally rewarding. Join me in doing something about it, starting today.

— *Lamar D. Berry*

INDEX

APPENDIX

The logos used in this book are the property of the respective companies
listed below:
Ben & Jerry's is the logo of Ben & Jerry's Homemade, Inc.
Chrysler is the logo of Chrysler Motors Corporation
Disney is the logo of The Walt Disney Company
Empress Riverboat Casino is the logo of Empress Casino Joliet
    Corporation
FedEx is the logo of FedEx
McDonald's is the logo of McDonald's Corporation
Nordstrom is the logo of Nordstrom, Inc.
Ritz-Carlton is the logo of Ritz-Carlton Hotel, Co.
Southwest Airlines is the logo of Southwest Airlines Company
Station Casinos is the logo of Station Casinos, Inc.
Texaco is the logo of Texaco Inc. (parent company for all Texaco
    subsidiaries)
Touro is the logo for Touro Infirmary